# ETHICS BOWL
# TO THE RESCUE!

## SAVING DEMOCRACY
### BY TRANSFORMING DEBATE

Matt Deaton, Ph.D.

# ETHICS BOWL
## TO THE RESCUE!
### SAVING DEMOCRACY BY TRANSFORMING DEBATE

by Matt Deaton, Ph.D.


Published by Notaed Press on International Democracy Day

Hardback ISBN 978-1-951677-15-2
Paperback ISBN 978-1-951677-16-9
eBook ISBN 978-1-951677-17-6

Paperback and Kindle editions available at Amazon.com. Bookstore, library, and bulk orders available through IngramContent.com.

Cover art by *Niezam*

SuperSocrates™ by J. Matt Deaton, but you're welcome to use him for pro-Ethics Bowl purposes for free with permission. Just email matt@mattdeaton.com to ask.

Back cover images courtesy of APPE IEB®, Ethics Olympiad, Mount Tamalpais College, and A2Ethics.

The views in this book represent those of the author at the time of writing, and do not necessarily reflect those of his employers nor any Ethics Bowl body including the Intercollegiate Ethics Bowl®, National High School Ethics Bowl, Ethics Olympiad, Ethics Bowl Canada, or Ethics Cup. This text was neither reviewed nor pre-approved by any institution or group, nor by people quoted or featured in photos. So for anything you don't like, kindly take it up with Matt.

For debaters.

JOIN US!

And for anyone who's ever
participated in, organized,
coached, judged, moderated,
or otherwise supported
an Ethics Bowl
aka Ethics Olympiad
aka Ethics Cup.

# ACKNOWLEDGMENTS

Thanks to the dozens of volunteers who took the time to answer interview questions for this book, as well as my generous beta readers: Michael Andersen, Lisa Deaton, Pat Hart, Richard Lesicko, J. Overton, and Court Lewis.

Thanks to Roberta Israeloff of the Squire Family Foundation for introducing me to Ethics Bowl at an Association for Practical and Professional Ethics meeting long ago, and for making possible the honor of serving as the original National High School Ethics Bowl Director of Outreach. Thanks also to Gary Squire for establishing the foundation and for supporting pre-college philosophy in such grand fashion.

Thanks to John Hardwig, mentor, friend, and retired University of Tennessee philosophy department chair for agreeing to fund the inaugural Tennessee High School Ethics Bowl, and for kindly persuading professors and grad students to support its launch and growth.

Thanks to Matthew Wills of Australia's Ethics Olympiad for the honor of serving as a judge and instructor, and for leading the global community with good cheer and grace.

Thanks to APPE IEB®, Ethics Olympiad, A2Ethics, and Mount Tamalpais College for permission to include photos.

And special thanks to Ethics Bowl creator Bob Ladenson and wife Joanne for your example, encouragement, and friendship. While our styles differ, everything offered here is shared with much admiration and respect.

# WHERE TO START

In **the U.S.** there's the Intercollegiate Ethics Bowl, National Bioethics Bowl, National High School Ethics Bowl, National Middle School Ethics Bowl, and Pan American Ethics Olympiad.

In **Australia, China, New Zealand, and India** there's the Ethics Olympiad, with options from elementary school through university.

Ethics Bowl **Canada** offers Collegiate and High School competitions, and there's also the Pan American Ethics Olympiad.

In the **United Kingdom** there's the Ethics Cup.

At least one school in the **Philippines,** one in **South Korea,** and one in **Iran** participates in Ethics Bowl, volunteers have brought Ethics Bowls into **prisons** in **at least five U.S. states**, and there's no reason ***you*** can't Ethics Bowl, too.

Visit **EthicsBowl.org/Resources** for a free "Ethics Bowl for the Classroom" guide or email **matt@mattdeaton.com** to discuss how to get involved.

No longer a student but still want to participate? Try **Ethics Slam!** covered in chapter 11.

And for all things Ethics Bowl, visit

**ETHICSBOWL.ORG**

# GIFT PROMO COPIES

If you're an Ethics Bowl organizer and would like to gift copies of this book to your coaches, judges, moderators, or participants (or use it to recruit new ones), a coach who would like to gift copies to your team (or potential team members), or otherwise would like to use *Ethics Bowl to the Rescue!* to promote and grow Ethics Bowl, email matt@mattdeaton.com from your institutional account to purchase copies at printing cost plus shipping (just shipping—we'll handle 'em for free). If you'd prefer to gift at-cost Kindle editions, we can do that—just email to discuss.

If you'd like to gift the PDF instead, and you think folks will be just as likely to read it in that format, no problem. Just email from your institutional address so we know the request is legit. Many kind Ethics Bowlers contributed to this project, and the more hands we can get it into, the more good it can do. You can even use the SuperSocrates character on the cover for pro-Ethics Bowl purposes for free. Just email and ask first, please.

Finally, if you're a coach or are considering coaching, I'd be happy to send you a copy of my *Ethics in a Nutshell: The Philosopher's Approach to Morality in 100 Pages*. It's available at Amazon and Audible, but also online in PDF and on audiobook (100 minutes) at EthicsBowl.org/Resources. Feel free to use the open online versions for anything related to Ethics Bowl, ethics, or philosophy.

Cheers,
Matt

# CONTENTS

# CHAPTER 1
# HUMILITY AS VICE

"In essence, it is about responsible free speech, the very cornerstone of our democracies."

– Estelle Lamoureux, Founder and Co-Organizer, Canadian High School Ethics Bowl

"As someone who works entirely in the area of ethics education, you could not ask for a better pedagogical tool."

– Kelly Laas, Former Co-Organizer, Chicago High School Ethics Bowl

"Ethics Bowl retains the benefits of traditional debate while offering something that is badly needed in the present moment."

– Michael Artime, Longtime Debate Coach and Intercollegiate Ethics Bowl Convert

A democratic ideal. An ethics educator's godsend. A superior debate alternative. With praise like this, why have so few even heard of Ethics Bowl? Because sometimes humility is a vice.

## We Got It from Our Daddy

Reserved, cordial, exceedingly kind—retired ethics professor Bob Ladenson's character is implicit in Ethics Bowl's expectations and embedded in its culture. The opposite of the cocksure arrogance rampant in politics and online, Ethics Bowl has quietly thrived as a beacon of enrichment excellence thanks largely to Bob's honorable example.

As Ethics Bowl's original creator, that much of the community would adopt his demeanor is understandable. Under normal circumstances, it would be laudable.

However, for a variety of reasons, democracy is in trouble. Tribalism, misinformation, and political violence are on the rise. While Ethics Bowl isn't a silver bullet, it has the power to help. But only if those of us who know speak up.

## Target Audiences

Accordingly, one goal of this book is to inspire existing Ethics Bowlers to become bolder champions. No more second-guessing Ethics Bowl's value. No more underselling its benefits. No more pretending it's just another extracurricular, no better than pickleball or 4-H. Modesty is usually a good thing. But we can't afford timidity and indecision—not in this climate. We possess a partial antidote to the rancor and hubris threatening the foundations of civil society. As serious students of morality, we know that passively watching a preventable tragedy is unacceptable.

Time to put the good of the many above our inhibitions.

That SuperSocrates character on the cover? That's every Ethics Bowl organizer, judge, moderator, case writer, and coach. That's *you!* Head up, shoulders back, rescue mode engaged.

UC SANTA BARBARA'S INTERCOLLEGIATE ETHICS BOWL TEAM DELIBERATING DURING THE CHAMPIONSHIP ROUND OF THE 2024 IEB NATIONALS *COURTESY OF APPE IEB®*

My second audience—arguably my most important audience—is the traditional debate community. Debaters, you're the reason we're here. My main purpose in writing this book has been to convince you to give Ethics Bowl a try. I think we have shared interests, I think Ethics Bowl is a better way to teach confidence and advocacy, and I think you'll find joining us enjoyable, easy, and more consistent with what you truly want. And with a robust infrastructure and overflowing expertise, all it will take are a few attitude and process shifts to begin transforming public discussion into a vehicle for solutions and peace.

Debaters, it's taken for granted that your motives have always been pure. You've had little reason to doubt that your model is anything but beneficial. But I'm not going to pull any punches when it comes to exposing debate's harms. This will be an unwelcome message at first. But I know you're open to quality argumentation, and so I'll be making a case that migrating to Ethics Bowl is the right thing to do. That case will include testimony from Ethics Bowl purists, but also from former debaters who've made the switch. Thank you for being open to the possibility that debate might stand room for improvement. Thank you for being open to trying Ethics Bowl.

So those are my primary audiences. But if you're neither an existing Ethics Bowler nor a debater, this book is also for anyone interested in elevating public discourse, promoting civic friendship and mutual respect. This isn't everyone. Experience suggests many (too many) prefer turmoil and drama. While I have great faith in humanity generally, we have to accept that some are locked in a tragic codependency with their perceived enemies.

But to my fellow solution-oriented ambassadors of compassion and goodwill, my goal is to gain your nod and assent. The drama-lovers have a great deal of power and attention at the moment. But we do not have to accept the status quo. The masses have unfortunately proven fickle, selfish, and irrational at least since the days of Socrates. It's our job to lead them out of this mess.

The good news is that the main thing you'll need to do is encourage friends and neighbors to check out the Ethics Bowl way.[1] Anytime someone brings up a traditional debate competition, kindly reply, "Have you tried Ethics Bowl?" With enough of us planting those seeds, the model will ultimately reach a critical mass and overtake attack-style debate organically.

## Moral Ambition

You may wind up convinced that Ethics Bowl can indeed save democracy, but unconvinced that you can do anything to help. "I'm not a coach. There's no way I could organize an event. Who would trust me to judge?"

Remember, you can simply spread the word. But I also want you to reflect on your skill set, your strengths, your connections, and your influence. Dutch historian Rutger Bregman makes a beautiful point in his 2025 international bestseller, *Moral Ambition: Stop Wasting Your Talent and Start Making a Difference*, that at every pivotal moment in history, when humankind elevated its standards and leapt forward,

1 Lend them this book or *The Ethics Bowl Way: Answering Questions, Questioning Answers, and Creating Ethical Communities*, edited by colleagues, friends, and longtime Ethics Bowl supporters Roberta Israeloff and Karen Mizell, Rowman & Littlefield, 2022.

it wasn't just spokesperson leaders who brought about the change, but thousands contributing behind the scenes.

> We often have a personal preference for a given type of activist: we may think protesters are brave and lobbyists useless; perhaps we have a weakness for poetic professors, but a distaste for slick influencers. Or vice versa.
>
> But change is not that one-dimensional. All these people can play an essential part. The intellectual and the influencer. The networker and the agitator. The bureaucrat and the entrepreneur. Someone who writes in academic jargon, someone who brings ideas to a wider public. Someone who's polarizing, someone who brings people together. Someone who lobbies behind the scenes, someone who lets themself get dragged away by the riot police.
>
> The only kind of person we can't use in this fight is the fool who thinks good intentions are enough. Someone whose clear-eyed convictions put them squarely on the right side of history, but who achieves little in the here and now. Let's call this figure the Noble Loser.[2]

That's what we want to avoid: knowing something needs to be done, being able to help, but deciding to hang

[2] Published by Little, Brown and Company, page 64.

back and watch—righteously scowling while the world burns.

Supporting Ethics Bowl, even in small ways, can save you from the terrible fate of drifting through life morally sincere, but feckless. "Noble Loser" is a bit harsh. But I hope it grabs your attention the way it grabbed mine.

Of course, there are other ways to improve the world. But Ethics Bowl is an especially easy, fun, and impactful path to meaningful change. You be the judge. But if you're convinced, don't talk yourself out of helping. For Bregman is right. We need all types.

AN ETHICS OLYMPIAD TEAM IN AUSTRALIA
DIFFERENT NAME, SAME EVENT, THOUGH ALMOST ALWAYS VIA ZOOM - COURTESY OF ETHICS OLYMPIAD

## Hard as a *What?*

To repeat, existing Ethics Bowlers: it's time to turn down the niceties and turn up the bullhorn. Respectfully, of course. But if you're like most I know, full-throated bragging does not come naturally. So to blunt what will be an unabashedly and fully deserved flatter-fest, and to head off any misconception that we're a bunch of prude know-it-alls, here's a quick story affirming our imperfections, beginning with my own.

Before Elon Musk chainsawed AmeriCorps, a small federal agency that provides grants to nonprofits and promotes public service, I had worked as a fulltime civil servant for over thirteen years. While I didn't ask to be laid off, it did allow me to finally finish this book. So, thank you, Elon, "Big Balls," and other classy patriots. Perhaps I'm contributing more to society outside of government after all.

Part of my time with the feds was in our nation's capital. I had used my free time to launch the inaugural Tennessee High School Ethics Bowl while in philosophy grad school at the University of Tennessee, so when I became a Presidential Management Fellow and moved the family just north of D.C. in 2012, I decided to use the same game plan to launch a Bowl there.

Thanks to support from the Squire Family Foundation and volunteers from American University, Georgetown University, and George Washington University, it worked. Georgetown and GW supplied judges, and American went all in, agreeing to sponsor, co-organize, and provide space.

Since I was in D.C., I invited members of Congress to judge or simply observe. My day job at the time was with the Congressional Research Service on Capitol Hill, so visiting the Senate and House office buildings down the street to hand out fliers during lunch was easy. Most politicians showed little interest. But one, a retired Republican congresswoman from Maryland, agreed to judge.

As a small-town kid from rural Tennessee, this was all very cool. I'd seen these places and people on television and in movies my whole life. Being in the middle of it was inspiring.

And as a citizen fed up with the acrimony of American politics, the potential of bringing Ethics Bowl to its epicenter was thrilling. My dissertation had been on public reasoning and the power of cooperative deliberation. I dreamed of transforming public discourse. This is where those changes were most needed and could do the most good.

But it was also nerve-racking. Hosting a new Bowl on my home turf had been manageable. But here, in this land of suits and power, I worried that my philosophical idealism would not be well received.

My saving grace: co-organizer and American University professor Ellen Feder. Thanks in large part to Ellen's charisma, connections, and persistence, we successfully recruited public schools, charter schools, private schools—even a school from Langley, Virginia, home of CIA headquarters, proving that even professional spies' kids can do ethics. Ellen handled the auditorium rental logistics, tapped AU philosophy grad students to moderate, and everything fell into place.

On Bowl day, despite being more anxious than usual, things went surprisingly well. The wrong judges' packet may have been sent to the wrong room once. But otherwise, the inaugural D.C. Area High School Ethics Bowl was a hit.

After a satisfying but long day of coordination, I hurriedly compiled final scores and rushed to the main auditorium where everyone was awaiting the results. Grabbing the mic and calling the room to order, I built some showman's anticipation and announced that the winner of the very first D.C. Area HSEB was... *School A!*

Everyone cheered and School A's coach accepted the first-place trophy with a beaming smile. Moments later, I was approached by a calm but puzzled coach from a different team—a coach who had taken the time to use their phone's calculator—a coach who kindly informed me that the winner was actually School *B.* We ran the numbers together. He was unfortunately correct.

An awkward announcement was made. School A's coach awkwardly conceded the trophy. School B's coach awkwardly took possession. And I'm pretty sure the only reason I was invited back was that I was the co-organizer.

Luckily, I was forgiven and hosted the D.C. Bowl again in 2013, this time meddling parents openly triple-checking my math. Fewer mistakes were made, and that spring I escorted the winners from School Without Walls to the University of North Carolina for the Inaugural National High School Ethics Bowl. Imagine the excitement within the Ethics Bowl Community as that date approached. After years of planning, a first *National* HSEB—woohoo!

The team was a pleasure to accompany and represented the District with honor. However, they somehow convinced me it was cool to say the team would be going "ham," which they assured me stood for "hard as a *mug.*" I didn't understand the connection to mugs, but not current on urban youth lingo, went along with it. Maybe it had something to do with coffee and a caffeine boost... So, between rounds in the hallways, as I passed other proud organizers from across the country chaperoning their own champion teams, I'd point at them and say, "Watch out—my D.C. team is going *ham* today!"

I didn't understand why the team would giggle when I said this. Later I discovered the "m" in hard as a m______ does not stand for mug, but for a word frequently heard coming out of the mouth of Samuel L. Jackson. That's right, as in, "I've had enough of these (not coffee mug) snakes on this (not coffee mug) plane!"

If you share my sense of humor, you're smiling right now. But if you don't, and if you happen to be an Ethics Bowl organizer, judge, or coach, you may be worried a story like this might tarnish our reputation. I can empathize. At least one beta reader suggested I axe the mug thing and maintain a more professional tone. I truly get it. But I think that if we're going to win converts—and that's a primary aim of this book—any misperception of smug condescension has to go. Ethics Bowlers are ordinary folks who happened to have stumbled upon a uniquely transformative tool. We have senses of humor. Some of us curse, though almost never at an Ethics Bowl (intentionally, anyway). But the fact that we take ethics seriously and promote a more productive, peaceful decision-making model doesn't mean we're holier-than-thou killjoys.

At our core, we're compassionate optimists. But we're also realists. Our specialty is *applied* ethics. Like Socrates, we get our philosophical hands very dirty. And we're not fools. It's understood that given the current situation, Ethics Bowl can't singlehandedly save the world. But we do think it can help, and we do think the time to accelerate its growth has arrived.

## Why Now?

In case you haven't opened a news app lately (and I wouldn't blame you if you haven't), civic norms are collapsing. Behaviors we once associated with fragile or failing states—supposed leaders spreading misinformation, inciting division rather than unity, rewarding violence and encouraging it in others—are becoming increasingly normalized. Longstanding expectations about peaceful transfers of power, a shared commitment to factual reality, and a very limited role for the military within domestic borders are being abandoned.

That norms are freakishly askew isn't our imagination. Political scientist Barbara Walter argued in her 2022 bestseller *How Civil Wars Start: And How to Stop Them* that the U.S. technically isn't even a democracy anymore.

> The United States became an anocracy [somewhere between democracy and autocracy] for the first time in more than two hundred years. Let that sink in. We are no longer the world's oldest continuous democracy. That honor is now held by Switzerland, followed by New Zealand, and then Canada.[3]

I've heard the term "autocratic republic" floated, a hybrid regime where democratic institutions still exist, but are hollowed out by declining accountability, an unchecked executive, and a legislature incentivized more by party primaries than national interest.

In response, little is being done to reclaim what's being lost. Many of us seem understandably frozen. There's a widespread sense of helplessness, as if the scale and intensity of the problem has outpaced our ability to respond. Underneath the paralysis lies a growing undercurrent of mutual contempt—a worsening animosity with explosive potential. Retired general Stanley McChrystal argues that

3 Published by Crown, page 138.

part of the reason is that group intimidation has morphed from fear to resentment to seething hatred.

> Fear isolates. It pushes us into ideological bunkers, surrounding us only with those who think like us. And when fear festers, it mutates. What begins as anxiety turns into resentment. Resentment hardens into hatred. Hatred strips away our ability to see others as people. The result is a society riven by suspicion and hostility.[4]

Exactly why our society has become riven by suspicion and hostility is debatable. McChrystal suggests digital mob intimidation may be a contributor, but it can't be the whole story. The best I can gather is that demographic shifts are eroding favored groups' advantages, which is causing insecurity, which is driving backlash, which is fueling hyper-partisanship, which is serving as a proxy for a culture war, which is being amplified by mass addiction to social media. Now add to the mix the certainty-destroying power of generative Artificial Intelligence and we're living through an unsettling time indeed.

However, I'm only an amateur cultural anthropologist. So take my explanation for what it's worth. But professional historian Neil Howe argues in his 2023

[4] "Be Not Afraid," April 13, 2025. https://www.nytimes.com/2025/04/13/opinion/mcchrystal-fear-america.html

bestseller *The Fourth Turning is Here: What the Seasons of History Tell Us About How and When This Crisis Will End* that the volatility we're currently experiencing is part of a predictable rejuvenating cycle. Unfortunately, we're at the cycle step where everything (temporarily) falls apart. And according to Howe, the U.S. currently satisfies a morose checklist of countries on the verge of armed domestic conflict.

> Trust in the national government is in steep decline. Check. Respect for democratic institutions is weakening. Check. A heavily armed population has polarized into two evenly divided partisan factions. Check. Each faction embodies a distinctive ethnic, cultural, and urban-versus-rural identity. Each wants its country to become something the other detests. And each fears the prospect of the other taking power. Check, check, check.[5]

That's depressing, and alarmist, and compels me to stock up on toilet paper for some reason. But the cyclical theory of history Howe offers makes some sense.

It all has to do with how generations are shaped by the culture of their youth, which in turn shapes how those grown-up kids drive history once in charge. As Howe's theory goes, Boomers who grew up during the post-war

5 Published by Simon and Schuster, page 261.

affluence of the 50s and came of age during the cultural revolution of the 60s and 70s are today's visionaries—visionaries who happen to be pushing incompatible versions of what society should look like (many Ethics Bowl leaders are Boomers). Jaded latchkey Gen Xers are now society's pragmatic mid-managers (that's me, God help us). The once overprotected Millennials are today's primary producers and doers (who knew?). And the hypersurveilled, hyperconnected Gen Zers are predicted to serve as dutiful order-followers during a coming crisis, then inherit a time of relative peace and prosperity (lucky you, current students).

If the seasons of Anglo-American history unfold as they did before and after the American Revolution, before and after the Civil War, and before and after WWII, Howe argues the current instability is right on schedule. Soon some terrible apex will usher in a two-decade period of unity and prosperity, followed by a two-decade period of questioning unrest, followed by a two-decade period of accelerating unraveling, followed by another crisis. Rinse and repeat.

The logic is that while people who directly experience the horrors of total war or economic collapse work hard to prevent it, subsequent sheltered generations become increasingly arrogant, and hubris eventually leads to another tragedy. According to Howe, the bad news is that something big and awful is inevitable and near. But the reassuring news is that happy days are on the other side.

## Measured, Determined Optimism

Some might take this as license to hunker down and hope the good guys win. If crap is going to hit the fan anyway, and if we'll probably survive, why not buy some Bitcoin and wait things out? I'll tell you why. Because for one, Bitcoin is a pyramid scheme. And for another, awaiting an apex calamity to renew us in due course is lunacy, especially in the atomic age.

Howe actually agrees and argues that understanding the generational cycles obliges us to proactively help. Wherever we find ourselves, we should accept our power to make the best of a bad situation, use our influence to steer events through the least destructive path, and work with other forward-thinkers to set the stage for rebirth.

> We should help our community prepare to be strong in the coming spring while allowing the least possible suffering while the storms rage… Knowing the season, we can decide how we can best assist those around us. We may be a mother, a teenager, or a grandfather. We may be a CEO, a mechanic, a congressperson, an officer, or a nurse. Whatever our personal role, we want to ask ourselves: How should we perform that role so that the winter season turns out well?[6]

[6] Ibid, page 455.

One role that I hope you'll come to embrace is that of vocal Ethics Bowl proponent. Its ability to literally save the world is of course limited. A seasonal club activity can't possibly fix everything. All I'm saying is that it's a partial antidote. Maybe not necessary. Maybe not sufficient. But if respectful, reasoned deliberation is the bedrock of a wise democracy, and if we're marching through an age deeply in need of democratic wisdom, herein lies a partial cure.

Demagogues will still find an audience. Some will win elections. Some will abuse our institutions and warp our culture's sensibilities. Pendulums will swing, with or without us. But by showing the world how to think through difficult issues in good faith, with skill, humility, and courage, and by providing a forum where young leaders can practice and showcase the method, we'll be laying the foundation for a more solidified, flourishing, just humanity.

So let go of that negative voice whispering, "It'll never work." Of course it's not a sure thing. But unless you're acting on a better idea, climb aboard SuperSocrates's back and let's do this. For it's Ethics Bowl to the rescue!

# CHAPTER 2
# THE BASICS

Whether it's an Ethics Olympiad in Australia, an Ethics Cup in the UK, or an Ethics Bowl in the U.S., think of them as enlightened, collaborative discussions.[7] OK, so they're like debates… But the twist is that "for" and "against" positions are not assigned. Instead, teams are given the freedom to decide for themselves what makes the most sense, and tasked with making a reasoned, sincere case supporting their view.

The other innovation is that there's no need for teams to pretend they alone possess the perfect, unassailable truth. Admitting error is OK. Ceding points is OK. Even changing your mind is OK (gasp!). Thoughtfulness, listening, a desire to learn rather than dominate—these are the refreshingly novel norms of Ethics Bowl. Associated Press columnist Travis Loller offered the following contrast in his 2025

7 "Ethics Bowl" is its original name and most common in the U.S., Canada, and the Philippines. "Ethics Olympiad" began in Australia, though teams from China, New Zealand, and India compete today (one recently from Iran), with U.S. and other teams frequently joining (there's even a Pan-American "Ethics Olympiad"). The formats and rules are almost identical, and oftentimes the same cases are used. Luckily, materials and ideas are shared freely, which is testament to the sort of person Ethics Bowl attracts.

article, "From Debate to Dialogue: In a Contentious Era, 'Ethics Bowl' Offers Students a Gentler Alternative."[8]

> At the National Speech and Debate Tournament, two high school students take the stage. The first articulates the position he has been assigned to defend—people should have a right to secede from their government—and why it is correct. Another student, assigned the opposite position, begins to systematically tear down her opponent's views.
>
> A year later and 800 miles away, two teams of high school students convene at the University of North Carolina for the National High School Ethics Bowl finals. A moderator asks about the boundaries of discourse—when a public figure dies, how do you weigh the value and harm of critical commentary about their life?
>
> Teams have not been assigned positions. One presents their ideas. The opposing team asks questions that help everyone to think about the issue more deeply. No one attacks.

While Ethics Bowls may appear debate-like, the expectations are much loftier. That said, sometimes Ethics Bowl teams slip into debate mode. They're only human, and the combative habits of traditional debate are deeply

[8] May 5, 2025.

ingrained. But when coaches don't get the memo and train their teams to attack, they're the freaks. There are plenty of forums for verbal assault, unfortunately. But when you come to an Ethics Bowl, be ready to own your views. When you come to an Ethics Bowl, be ready to deliberate from the heart. When you come to an Ethics Bowl, be ready to adult.

If a pop culture character would help, my go-to example is Star Trek's Spock. Half Vulcan, his reasoning skill is impeccable. But half human, emotion and intuition are infused with his judgments. While Spock takes pride in his thinking abilities, his commitment to the truth combined with recognition of his fallibility compels him to remain forever open to changing his mind.

STANFORD UNIVERSITY'S IEB TEAM DELIBERATING IN THE CHAMPIONSHIP ROUND OF THE 2025 IEB NATIONALS

*COURTESY OF APPE IEB®*

For non-Trekkies, maybe think of Chidi from NBC's *The Good Place.* On second thought, don't. While seeing a handsome ethics professor star alongside the great Ted Danson on a hit TV show is quite the ego boost, Chidi's maddening indecisiveness disqualifies him as a model ethicist. Search YouTube for "Chidi trolley dilemma" to see why. Warning: blood!

And while I love and would suggest Yoda, his pithy Jedi aphorisms are far too cryptic. Philosophy requires articulating the *why.* "Do or do not, says wise Yoda. But explain why? The green master does not."

To succeed at Ethics Bowl, transparency, logical rigor, emotional intelligence, humility, and an eagerness to collaborate are helpful traits. But if a recruit doesn't possess these at first – good news – simply being involved will help bring them about. Ethics Bowl improves the people it touches. Not only participants, but organizers, judges, coaches, and moderators – ultimately even their schools, families, and communities. To begin to understand how, let's walk through a typical event.

## The Bowl Day Experience

University of West Georgia philosophy professor, Intercollegiate Ethics Bowl judge, and West Georgia High School Ethics Bowl organizer, Walter Riker (no relation *Star Trek: The Next Generation's* Commander William Riker, though equally adventurous and good-looking) summarizes the Ethics Bowl experience in three brief phrases:

> Listening to others and engaging in reciprocal reason-giving. Developing thoughtful, reasoned responses to moral problems. Working with others to solve common problems.

That sounds almost too pleasant to be true. But it is, though an actual Bowl unfolds much like other academic events.

Bowl day begins with check-ins and name tags. Newbies nervously chatter while veterans search for familiar faces. Team members sample fruit and pastries while coaches and judges top off their coffees. As the appointed time approaches, everyone gathers in the assembly room to receive the organizer's well wishes, thanks, and praise.

Judge assignments are confirmed—typically three per room when competing in person, sometimes fewer when via Zoom. Teams find out whom they'll face in the morning seeding rounds. As the mass disperses, coaches impart last-minute tips, moderators double-check their packets for adequate scratch paper and pencils, and everyone finds their way to their assigned room.

When the round begins, the moderator flips a coin to see who goes first, announces the first case and reads the first official question. The teams will have received a set of ten to fifteen cases and sample study questions months in advance. But they'll just be learning which case will be used in the first portion of this round, as well as the official question.

MARK DOORLEY OPENING A ROUND WITH THE COIN FLIP AT 2024 IEB NATIONALS, JUDGE TASNEEM SYEDA LOOKING ON
COURTESY OF APPE IEB®

Once the case and question are revealed, team A is given two to three minutes to huddle and confer. Their main thoughts will have been formed weeks ago. This is simply an opportunity to adjust their position per the specifics of the just-announced prompt and to confirm who's covering what.

A deep breath, and then up to five minutes to deliver their initial presentation. A captain can volunteer to handle the speaking, but more commonly the group of three-to-five team members will take turns.[9] Everyone remains seated. Team B observes and takes notes. So do the judges.

Judges listen for three main things: that the team's ideas are clear and coherent, that they're aware of and sensitive to the primary moral values in tension, and that the team is proactively responding to a reasonable objection to their view.

The first should be a gimmie. Cases are about a page each, and with months to prepare, any team that's had the interest and time should be able to demonstrate familiarity with key details and a basic ability to not self-contradict. Plus, between the sample study questions, study guides at EthicsBowl.org, and assistance from AI—a surprisingly helpful case analysis aid, though no replacement for organic human insight[10]—there's little excuse for not nailing box one on the judges' score sheets.

Box two is tougher. Ethics Bowl cases intentionally pit legitimate interests against legitimate interests, core values against core values, shared moral intuitions against shared moral intuitions. One main case character may have the most to lose. One line of reasoning may seem most promising. But if a particular judgment appears obviously irrefutable, look again.

Case committees craft dilemmas (sometimes trilemmas, sometimes multi-lemmas) that could be

9 Rules vary, so team size can differ depending on the event.
10 More on the promise and risks of AI in chapter 10.

reasonably decided many ways. Part of being a mature moral reasoner is casting a wide net, of taking seriously all impacted parties, not simply whichever character you happen to empathize with most. Declaring a supremely important protagonist and a single overarching perspective belies a superficial understanding and failure to self-challenge. Judges want breadth and depth. And just like math teachers, they expect to see (or in this case, hear) teams' work, which means sharing high points from the pre-Bowl discussions that ultimately led to their view. Judges want to hear that teams ultimately settled on view X. But they also want to understand how they got there.

Last, judges are listening for whether a team concedes how a reasonable person could disagree with them, as well as how they might respond. This proactive consideration of an objection is standard in academic philosophy, yet it's where many teams lose easy points, probably because it's so rare in daily life. We're so conditioned to expect conceited one-sidedness that for many it feels taboo—unthinkably generous—to concede how a non-moron could ever disagree with us. Were most politicians to admit how a smart and kind critic might be justified in disagreeing with their policy proposal, we'd be shocked. But quality self-analysis is the expectation, and teams that fail to demonstrate it are both unlikely to impress the judges and are more open to penetrating critique during Team B's turn.

## Team B's Commentary and Team A's Reply

All of the above occurs in the opening portion of a round. Once Team A finishes, Team B confers, shares notes, and prepares their commentary. The use of "commentary" rather than "rebuttal" is intentional.

Unique to Ethics Bowl, Team B isn't required to discredit or attack Team A. In fact, overt hostility or rudeness can cost a team points. Judges are listening for Team B to expand the conversation and enrich participants' understanding. Unlike traditional debate, Team B is welcome to affirm what Team A said, so long as they meaningfully further the discussion.

Of course, simply praising Team A would be transparently lazy. If Team A has done a great job, Team B could very well agree with them and struggle to articulate a rejoinder with philosophical gravitas. However, as Ethics Bowl creator Bob Ladenson explains, there's always something to add.

> Even if [the commenting team] agrees with the presenting team's conclusions, for example, the commenting team can discuss aspects of the presenting team's reasoning it finds problematic. Furthermore, even if it considers the presenting team's analysis persuasive, the commenting team can develop another analysis which highlights other morally significant considerations. The mark of an excellent commentary is the contribution it makes to

meaningful and productive communication.[11]

Criticism is certainly allowed. It's not like Team B is expected to give crummy arguments a pass for the sake of politeness. Rather, the idea is to encourage a spirit of cooperative discovery, in the hope that by working together, the understanding of everyone in attendance will be improved. As Bob puts it, commentary worthy of high judges' scores facilitates "meaningful and productive communication." And this is of course very different from the expectations of traditional debate, where the idea is to dominate and destroy, independent of whether you privately believe another's position truly makes more sense.

## Judge Q&A

Once Team B delivers its commentary and Team A responds, the mood shifts. Coaches cross their arms, parents flee to the hallway, teams shrink in their seats. Breaking from the otherwise collegial norm, the judges mercilessly badger Team A until at least one member cries. Yes, until one cries. Often this is the youngest participant, victim of an initiation of sorts. But regardless of who breaks, Team B looks away while the moderator mocks them and jubilant spectators whip the crybaby with hemlock.

[11] "Reflections on the Intercollegiate Ethics Bowl," *The Philosopher's Magazine*, Nov 15, 2022

I'm kidding! Ethics Bowl judges are some of the kindest, most compassionate, tactful, morally mindful people you'll meet. They do ask tough questions. But the idea isn't to tear teams down, but to inspire deeper thought. A common strategy is to change some aspect of the case and ask the team whether and how their judgments might change were key details different. Another is to press a team to more thoroughly address a challenge raised by the other team during the commentary portion.

Good judges inject a seasoned perspective. They've not only pre-read the case set, but have studied, written or at least read professional articles on the topics. Superb judges have been leading students through related philosophical territory for years. Being a tenured ethics professor isn't necessary. Most Bowl organizers, especially on the younger levels, strive to recruit judges from a variety of backgrounds, and moral wisdom requires no philosophical training. But rounds are usually more productive when at least one ethics professional is on the judging panel. Professors with experience teaching applied ethics can better anticipate fruitful lines of inquiry, have more practice segregating their personal convictions from their teaching role, and can better distinguish genuine ethical insight from an eloquent bluff.

Done well, judge Q&A exposes teams who've memorized scripted responses prepared by a coach or a chatbot rather than doing the work themselves. Do they really understand the intricacies of Utilitarianism? Or are they simply namedropping J.S. Mill? Sometimes this is obvious from an initial presentation or commentary reply. But the unspoken purpose of judge Q&A isn't simply to probe and confirm which teams truly embody Ethics Bowl's intended virtues, but to take the discussion to the next level. Teams with good coaches will have made much progress during preparation. But the expectation is that the event itself will expand teams' understanding even further. And while back and forth between the teams does this some, the judges are there to challenge assumptions, model deeper inquiry, and help the teams develop more nuanced, defendable conclusions.

## A Virtuous Conspiracy

Once Team A's judge Q&A period is over, the roles swap. Now it's Team B's turn. They're given a different case and question, they confer and provide their initial response, Team A confers and shares commentary, Team B confers and responds, then Team B fields their own judges' questions.

Everyone exhales while the judges' score sheets are tallied. Usually, whichever team receives the most judges' votes wins the round. But with some variants, such as Ethics Olympiad, a running point total determines gold, silver, and bronze medal awards at the end of the day. Either way, once a round is completed, the teams move on by either physically walking to another room or virtually jumping on another Zoom, where they'll face a different team, different cases, different questions, and different judges.

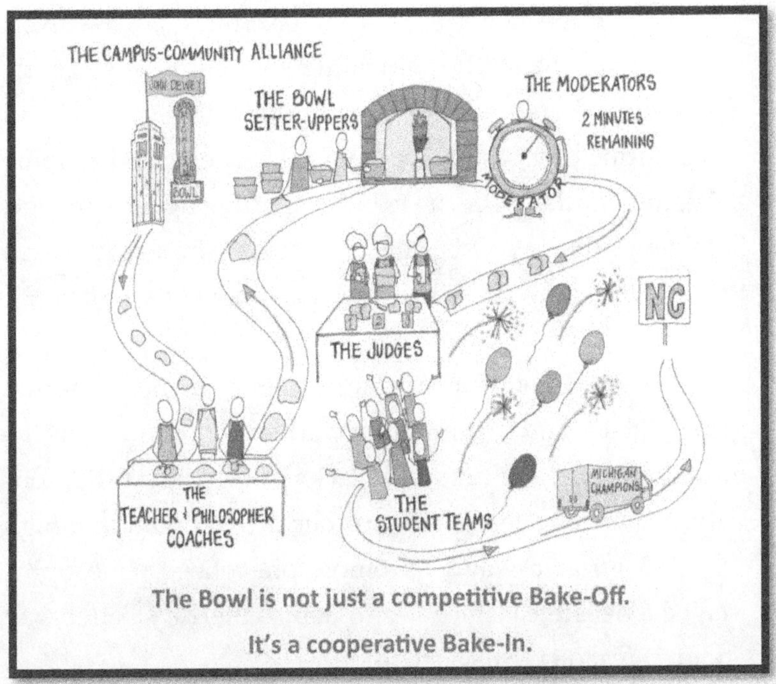


**BOWL FLOW ILLUSTRATION BY ARTIST DUSTY UPTON OF A2ETHICS AND THE MICHIGAN HIGH SCHOOL ETHICS BOWL** *COURTESY OF A2ETHICS*

From the outside, you might think all this runs on autopilot. In reality, it's the product of extensive planning and pre-work. Ethics Bowl case committees take pains to articulate scenarios lacking obvious solutions. Organizers word competition questions to maximize response value. Judges probe with expert intention, striving to strike a balance that's instructive, but not too leading—challenging, but still affirming.

Coaches—the true heroes of Ethics Bowl—invest untold hours patiently cultivating thoughtfulness, gently challenging sacred assumptions, illuminating moral blind spots, luring shy students out of their shells, and helping boisterous students see the value of shutting up for a change. Sometimes the payoff is slow. But those who've witnessed the growth know it will come and know it's worth the trouble.

Thousands of members of a diverse and dispersed global Ethics Bowl community play a part, adding to the movement's momentum with each new volunteer. Reasons vary. Maybe a college professor decides to organize a high school Bowl as a way to promote pre-college philosophy. Maybe a debate coach comes to realize there's a better way and decides to give us a try (hint!).

But the ambition that continues to inspire so many is that over time, Ethics Bowl's humility, thoughtfulness, cooperation, and mutual respect will spread from participant to family to community to legislative body, in the process replacing lower-rung combative tribalism with higher-order collaborative justice. Many are simply sick of petty cruelty masquerading as strength and have decided to build something that models and rewards decency instead. More on Ethics Bowlers' motivations in chapter 4: Why They Do It.

Ok, so that's the Ethics Bowl experience in a nutshell. But here are answers to a few frequently asked questions.

## Do Teams Have to Invoke Ethical Theory?

There's zero requirement that teams use ethical theory. As Ethics Bowl pioneer Pat Croskery used to say, "It's *Ethics* Bowl, not *Theory* Bowl."[12] And unless you're prepared to explain deontology, don't bring it up by that fancy name (moral duties will do). Correctly pronouncing Kant might intimidate the other team. But it might also tempt judges to test your German. If a team truly understands Kant's Categorical Imperative, great. But common sense, everyday morality is more than adequate.

[12] Pat is a big reason Ethics Bowl is as successful, warm, and fun as it is today. He passed away in 2019 at the age of 58 after a brief and courageous battle with cancer, and IEB honors him each season by awarding an exemplary coach or team sponsor the Pat Croskery Memorial Award. From the IEB website, "Pat was loved and admired by all who knew him. He had a way of living that put ethics at the forefront at all times, and involved an approach to interactions with others that exemplified respect for persons no matter what their views, combined with a commitment to civil discourse. For Pat almost any problem could be solved, and all issues could be resolved, by carefully listening to the needs of those involved, and finding a way for all to be satisfied. People in the Ethics Bowl community routinely sought Pat's counsel as he could be counted on to provide accurate and unbiased, yet compassionate feedback. As a teacher he was dedicated to students realizing the full value of the Ethics Bowl experience, which was not just about participating in an exciting competition, but about gaining respect for competing viewpoints, developing lifelong moral reasoning skills, and learning how to discuss complicated moral issues with those who hold different views in a way that serves to better society. Pat was a true mentor to many."

While I cover the four dominant ethical theories in my college classes, when I teach younger audiences, such as Junior Ethics Olympiad trainees, I'll frame the ideas plainly—talk about character rather than Virtue Ethics, relationships rather than Care Ethics, consequences rather than Utilitarianism, consistency and respect rather than Kantianism. Ethics Olympiad organizer Matthew Wills wisely requests this approach when he invites speakers to avoid scaring away new *eth-letes* (he calls Ethics Olympiad participants "eth-letes" as in "ethics athletes"—isn't that awesome!), and it's worked fantastically well.

## Are Team Members Always from the Same School?

Teams usually represent a single school or university. This is usually mandated in the official rules. But this isn't always the case, especially with independent events.

For example, in years' past, the East Texas High School Ethics Bowl hosted by UT-Tyler (where I proudly teach as an online adjunct) brought together and mixed students from different schools as a leadership exercise. Today, the University of North Florida, which also hosts both the Southeast IEB regional and the North Florida (First Coast) HSEB, holds an Ethics Academy summer camp culminating "in a mini Ethics Bowl competition, where groups of students will discuss the cases that they have developed over the course of the summer camp."[13]

Another example: the Ethics Olympiad in Australia, Ethics Bowl Canada, and the National High School Ethics Bowl all officially allow homeschool teams made up of students from different families. Sometimes these teams are quite good. Triangle Homeschool, a talented group from North Carolina, took third place at the inaugural National High School Ethics Bowl in 2013. I was there, and recall being very impressed. Dr. Sam Rocha, a philosophy of education professor at the University of British Columbia in Canada and editor-in-chief of *Philosophy in Education,* coaches the Distributed Learning Homeschool Group, most of the members of which have belonged to a homeschool cooperative since 2014. In 2024, his team won the Democracy in our Backyard tournament and became co-champion of their regional, then went on to compete in the 2025 Canadian high school nationals.

> We started as a teen reading group, reading some of Plato's Dialogues together. After volunteering as a judge, I presented the option to the team to compete and we prepared by continuing to study primary

[13] UNF's ethics outreach work is coordinated by the Florida Blue Center for Ethics, directed by UNF philosophy professor Jonathan Matheson. They even host Philosophy Slams (we'll talk about Ethics Slams in chapter 11). Nice work, UNF!

texts in moral philosophy. After we qualified for nationals, we studied Shelley Kagan's *Normative Ethics* as our preparation.

Rocha's team's success may in part be due to their demanding prep, but it might also be due to the fact that two of his kids, Tomas and Gabriel, are on his team. This fall, if things work out, I'll be coaching a high school team with two of my kids, senior Justin and freshman Emily. However, we will not be reading Plato. Justin tried Plato's *Republic* when he was younger, and it almost turned him away from philosophy for life.

So, while unified school teams are the norm, there are exceptions, especially on the high school level, which are coordinated with regional organizers, who coordinate with national organizers. And assign Plato to 10-year-olds at your own risk (he's 17 now, but I'm afraid to try again).

## Do Teams Always Get Cases in Advance?

Teams usually have several months to reflect on the case set, work with coaches, and prepare their views. But some Bowls have recently introduced a twist—presenting teams with a brand-new case late in the day.

Some events only do this during bonus consolation rounds with no impact on the outcome. However, testing teams' ability to reason on the fly might be a great way to up the stakes for championship rounds, and at least two high school Bowls in the Northwest recently started introducing new cases in round 3. More on innovations to make Ethics Bowl even better in chapter 9: Ethics Bowl's Future.

## Do Teams Ever Interact Directly?

Ethics Bowl discussion has always been direct during the judges' Q&A. But the model has traditionally kept teams carefully sequestered, at least until the end, when smiles, mutual thanks, and handshakes are typical while final scores are tabulated. But during the round, while one team speaks, the other listens. Not only are interruptions during delivery banned, only one team is permitted to communicate verbally during the conferral periods. The other team can pass notes, but that's it. Usually, there's no live team-to-team interaction.

On the one hand, this promotes a very high order of respect. On the other, it's completely unrealistic.

However, some organizers are experimenting with live back-and-forth. Initial results are inconclusive. But I welcome the innovation and think that if anyone can make that work, it's Ethics Bowlers. Again, stay tuned for innovations in chapter 9.

## Even Better, Watch One

So those are the basics. Similar to debate, but with minor tweaks in attitude that make a huge difference in impact. The best way to appreciate the differences is to watch one, and several examples are available on YouTube.

Even better, attend one. No one's going to turn you away if you show up as a spectator. Just search your area + Ethics Bowl and reach out to me if you're having trouble figuring out when and where to be.

And if you'd like to experience the next best thing and happen to live near Michigan or Utah, look up Ethics Slam. More on Ethics Slam in chapter 11: Early, After, and Beyond Academia.

But first, I've talked quite a bit of anti-debate smack without clearly explaining why. So we now turn to why traditional debate is so bad and Ethics Bowl the logical, virtuous alternative. I'm not going to pull many punches, so if you've been a diehard debater, this will initially sting. But know that I offer the critique as an act of liberating love, in the spirit of a prisoner who's escaped Plato's cave and is eager to liberate his comrades, whether they're ready or not.

# CHAPTER 3
# > DEBATE

When Richard Lesicko began coaching competitive speaking teams in 1975, the National Debate Tournament was the default option. Today there's the Cross-Examination Debate Association, the National Parliamentary Debate Association, the World Parliamentary Debate Association, the National Forensic Association's Lincoln-Douglas Debate, the Collegiate Public Forum Debate League, the Public Communication Speech and Debate League, the National Educational Debate Association, the International Public Debate Association, and more. But in 2010, coach Richard was enticed to try something called Ethics Bowl, initially to save time and money.

> Any form of debate is an expensive proposition. To be competitive, one needs to attend a certain number of invitational tournaments before regional qualifiers and/or the national tournament. Ethics Bowl has a simple travel schedule: there is the regional qualifier and, if one is both good and lucky, a trip to nationals.

While IEB teams are technically allowed to compete in multiple regionals, Richard found this was less common in Ethics Bowl than in debate, which lessened richer teams' ability to rack up an experience edge. Ambitious coaches are welcome to arrange scrimmages. And some IEB programs are known for competing in multiple regionals, some even splitting their members to compete in different regionals on the same weekend. But with Ethics Bowl, Richard didn't consider a paltry travel budget an insurmountable disadvantage the way it can be with traditional debate.

Time, cost, and fairness were the initial draws. But as his team acclimated to Ethics Bowl's norms, Richard was surprised by how the format tended to better develop public speakers.

> Whether by design or luck, Ethics Bowl is a damn good cure for ordinary communication apprehension. Students are more comfortable delivering their message while they are seated, more comfortable sharing the load with a group of people as opposed to standing all alone in front of the judges, and more comfortable having to deliver only part of the ten-minute presentation.

Indeed, students not yet comfortable speaking can contribute during Bowl prep or conferral periods, then grow into an oratory role at their own pace. Debate, on the other hand, typically demands all participants speak competently, and usually combatively, on day one. Andy Cullison, Executive Director of the Cincinnati Ethics Center and member of DePauw University's inaugural Ethics Bowl team in 1999, makes a similar point in *The Ethics Bowl Way.*

> In debate and similar events, students are often required to stand up and speak, by themselves, in front of spectators. For a shy student, this can feel like being tossed into the deep end of the pool and told to start swimming. Ethics Bowl, with its focus on teams, consensus building, and carefully planned structure, gives all students the opportunity to make micro-contributions at first and gradually assume larger roles.[14]

In addition to better teaching public speaking, the more Richard coached, the more apparent it became that Ethics Bowl better prepared students for real conversations. Sure, debaters were exposed to a range of issues, they expanded their understanding of those issues, and developed confidence talking about them. But in the real world, debate tactics can be not only offputting, but downright counterproductive.

> Debaters learn things that do not serve them well in later life. Within the confines of the tournament, there is pressure to overwhelm your opponent with more arguments than they can answer in the time

14 Chapter 8, "Beyond Argument: Learning Life Skills Through Ethics Bowl," page 68.

> allowed. Invariably, debaters opt to surround their good arguments with a flurry of bad arguments... When a college hosts a debate tournament, the host does not invite their president or provost to judge a round. More than one program has lost its funding because a senior administrator has wandered the halls of a tournament and heard teams spewing arguments at more than 300 words per minute.

In sum, Richard found Ethics Bowl to be more affordable and less labor-intensive than traditional debate. He found it better at easing students into speaking roles. And he concluded Ethics Bowl avoids debate's rapid-fire overwhelm tactics that tend to self-destruct in the real world.

Michael Artime, political science professor at Pacific Lutheran University in Tacoma, Washington, also comes from the world of traditional debate. He was a policy debater in high school and went on to coach and judge parliamentary debate on the college level. But last year he had the opportunity to help host the Northwest IEB regional and coach Pacific Lutheran's IEB team.

While Artime had admired Ethics Bowl from afar for some time, he came away with a heightened awareness of traditional debate's tendency to encourage mercenary-like manipulation, and an increased appreciation for Ethics Bowl's emphasis on sincerity and respect. Given the devolving political climate in which we find ourselves, Artime concluded that Ethics Bowl's approach was far more needed. So with his direct experience with both formats, I asked him what he would say to traditional debaters intrigued by Ethics Bowl.

> My pitch to those considering the switch would be this: Debate has been an indispensable part of my growth as an academic. I learned critical thinking, the development of strong arguments, and communication skills that I use every day. However, these activities prioritized winning and a kind of moral ambivalence as you prepare to make any argument that might help you accomplish that goal. Ethics Bowl retains the benefits of traditional debate while offering something that is badly needed in the present moment.
>
> In an age in which democratic principles, rights, and human dignity are often under attack, we need to equip students to live principled lives. This happens in an environment that fosters collaborative dialogue rather than divisiveness. Ethics Bowl rewards deep thinking and clarity over strategic maneuvers. The conversations are less about how to develop a winning strategy and more about how we can find an ethical response to each case that is consistent with the commitments of the group. Ethics Bowl presents an invaluable opportunity for our students to develop as thinkers and principled members of

> their communities. The respectful, cooperative nature of the activity is unlike anything that I have seen in other forms of debate. If our local, national, and global leaders participated in this activity, I have no doubt that the level of discourse that permeates so much of our politics would be vastly improved.

## Eloquent Bullies

To be clear, both Artime and Lesicko continue to hold traditional debate in high regard. However, while debate has its benefits, the problem is that it conditions participants to accept and attack rather than discern and decide. Apart from the meanspiritedness and yelling, debate's practice of assigning teams for or against positions teaches a militaristic deference. "Team A, you're for it. Team B, you're against it. Do not question your orders. Now, fight!"

I admit that the performative hostility and drama of no-holds-barred verbal combat can be entertaining. But it's ultimately a lowbrow spectacle unworthy of educators' consent, let alone our endorsement and support. It would be bad enough if debate only produced snarky coworkers and internet trolls. But it's a corruptor of our most promising future leaders. It's a contributor to our increasingly fat-fisted political culture. And it's an institution in need of drastic reform.

When students are told what to think, trained to unflinchingly defend what they've been told to think, invited to use rhetorical trickery, punished for second guessing themselves, forbidden from changing their minds—belligerent hubris is a predictable result.

If you're a debater, you undoubtedly believe the practice is worthwhile. But ask yourself, does traditional debate encourage civic friendship? Does it model admirable leadership? Does it inspire a solution-oriented, sincere pursuit of objective justice? Or does it teach unquestionable acceptance of divisive dogma, reflexive demonization of anyone who disagrees, and an adversarial posture undermining solidarity and trust?

For an individual example, consider the perspective of Sona Zarkou of the 2025 NHSEB championship-winning BASIS High School team from Flagstaff, AZ. As reported by Travis Loller for the Associated Press.

> When [Sona] practiced debate, she says, she was "kind of a jerk"—"very quick to attack and very rude" about opposing views. In Ethics Bowl she sees herself "turn the discussion to something a lot more respectful, a lot more truth-oriented."[15]

For a broader example with modest data, consider the findings of professors who studied 165 high school students brought together in D.C. to discuss social issues as part of the Close Up Washington civics education program.

15 "From Debate to Dialogue: In a Contentious Era, 'Ethics Bowl' Offers Students a Gentler Alternative," May 5, 2025.

Some groups held traditional assigned-position competitive debates, while others earnestly deliberated in Ethics Bowl-like discussions.

Those engaged in more open discussion started out divided, but moved toward principled agreement over the course of the sessions. However, those engaged in more traditional debate became even more divided. As North Carolina State professor Paula McAvoy said in the study:

> The value of deliberation is it can promote an openness to changing your mind and being persuaded... In our highly polarized climate, do we want kids to become more entrenched in their views, or more open to learning about the issues? These findings can help teachers decide which skills they want students to learn, depending on how they structure classroom discussions.[16]

Educators exercise an enormous influence which accumulates over our students' academic careers. Anytime our classes discuss a hot topic, whether informally or in a structured setting, we can reinforce the expectation that they

[16] Study title: "Divisions? Evidence from a Study of High School Students" by Drs. Greg and Paula McAvoy, *Peabody Journal of Education*, Volume 96, Issue 3, 2021. Overview article: "Political Discussions Focused on Consensus More Comfortable, Less Divisive for Students" by Laura Oleniacz for North Carolina State's website, July 27, 2021.

should quickly divide into factions and battle. Or we can make subtle shifts that teach them that the mature approach is to listen, seek mutual understanding, and work together.

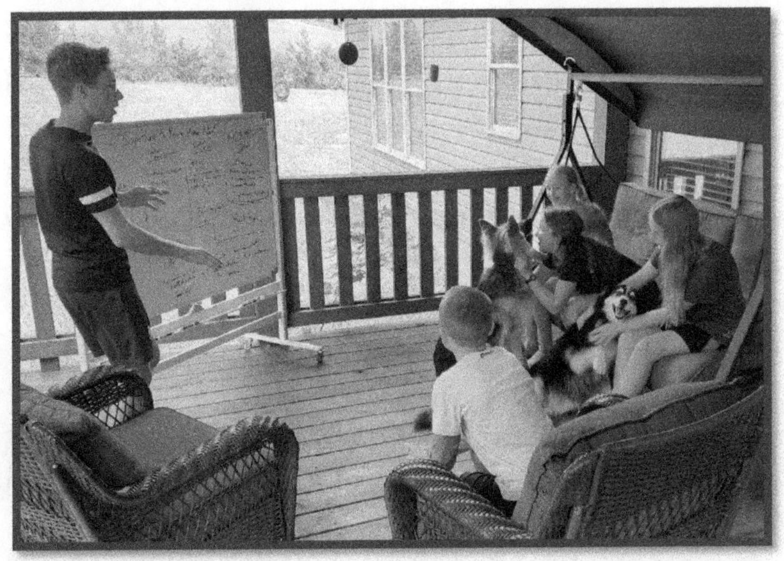

A TEAM DISCUSSES A NHSEB CASE ON THEIR COACH'S BACK PORCH
*COURTESY OF MY BACK PORCH*

The instinct to "win" is understandable. In some contexts—like an actual courtroom—it's appropriate. But courtrooms are strictly managed environments, overseen by a judge and decided by a jury. The adversarial norms that work within the legal system, extended into every conversation, rob us of our ability to combine our wisdom. Outside of that narrow context, a lawyer-like attitude of zealous advocacy poisons what could otherwise be a productive conversation. If we want to see more admirable discussions among our leaders and across our culture, shifting from traditional debate to Ethics Bowl is part of the answer.

## The Virtue of Inhospitality

One might worry that pushing consensus could make participants more vulnerable to manipulation. This is true. If you and I begin with the goal of reaching agreement and you trust me to reason in good faith, but I'm secretly pushing a predetermined agenda, I could steer you towards a conclusion that ignores your interests, conflicts with your values, and takes you somewhere you wouldn't voluntarily go. You could do the same to me.

However, Ethics Bowl is not about consensus. It's about reason-giving and the collaborative pursuit of moral enlightenment. If an argument is bad, it's our duty to say so—respectfully, of course. Sometimes people mean well but are simply wrong, and other times they're knowingly misleading. But either way, adopting an inferior view or splitting the difference between extremes is an unlikely path to moral progress.

To be clear, in Ethics Bowl, and in academic philosophy generally, there's zero pressure to appease bad arguments. Everyone deserves to be heard and thoughtfully addressed. But Socrates didn't bow to flawed reasoning just to keep the peace, and he didn't pretend that any old opinion was as good as the next—even when his life was at stake.

In a journal article I often assign in my Ethics Intro classes, Rochester Institute of Technology philosophy professor Lawrence Torcello argues that citizens in democracies have an obligation to discuss public policy in a fact-driven, mutually respectful way, and to confront people who deviate from that norm. [17] When leaders invoke debunked claims, astrology, or preposterous conspiracies, it's not OK to look the other way. In fact, Torcello argues that when we engage in "complicit hospitality" and give BS a free pass, we're partially responsible for resulting harms.

After all, citizens in a democracy collectively drive their country's policies. And the duty to speak up is especially incumbent upon those with disproportionate influence, including journalists, scientists, clergy, public intellectuals, and educators. Torcello invokes the ghost of Socrates, who was sentenced to death for speaking truth to power, to implore philosophers in particular.

> If this seems like a large moral burden, it should be weighed against the still-greater burden of living with the consequences of unchecked pseudoscience, science denialism, and political demagoguery.[18]

17 "On the Virtues of Inhospitality: Toward an Ethics of Public Reason and Critical Engagement," PHILO Vol. 17, No. 1, Spring-Summer 2014.

18 Ibid, page 111.

While cordiality and openmindedness are encouraged, neither philosophy nor Ethics Bowl provide safe harbor for sloppy reasoning. Plus, while convergence is nice when it happens, it's taken for granted that on almost all issues, full consensus will never come. Harvard political philosopher John Rawls wrote extensively about how reasonable disagreement was an unavoidable fact. Equally intelligent people with the same information will continue to arrive at conflicting conclusions on big questions including questions concerning the ultimate nature of the universe, the meaning of life, and tough moral and political issues. The reason: what Rawls called the "burdens of judgment."

Apart from our imperfect intellects, our thinking is clouded by our life experiences and distorted by our quirks. While we may think we have an issue fully figured out, and we may think everyone would agree if only they'd listen, persistent disagreement is certain due to the human condition. This remains true even when others share our commitment to the truth, are just as diligent, and just as smart.

Realizing as much can be disheartening at first. But it's reality, and the good news is that while 100% agreement is impossible, progress can be made—meaning that by working together, we can all better align with the objectively best views, whatever they might be. And that's darn sure more likely to happen when we're following Ethics Bowl's model rather than traditional debate's.

The reason is that while Ethics Bowl is humble enough to concede that we all have room for improvement, debate teaches that the answers are already known, and all that's left to do is beat the opposition into submission. If this attitude were isolated to a school activity, we might overlook it. But when your culture is conditioned by debate's "receive and blindly defend" mentality, genuine discussion becomes vanishingly rare. For tribes already inclined to believe they possess the inerrant truth, the goal is to impose rather than engage. Rather than combining our wisdom to find solutions, we mutually destroy. But it doesn't have to be this way.

Debate's culture of over-the-top aggression and forced closemindedness leaves much to be desired. To be blunt, debate produces eloquent bullies, foot soldiers ready to receive an ideology and deploy. This is the opposite of what the world needs, and unworthy of thoughtful educators' support. I see little reason to cling to such a counterproductive, poisonous approach, especially when there's a far better, easily adoptable alternative.

## Kinder Voices

Francesca Hovagimian, former University of California Santa Cruz Intercollegiate Ethics Bowl team member, volunteer high school Ethics Bowl coach and moderator, Ethics Bowl judge at San Quentin (yes, the prison—more in chapter 12: Bowls Behind Bars?) and Las Vegas attorney, explains the contrast more diplomatically.

> I think Ethics Bowl's primary benefit is that it presents morally complex and relevant issues for discussion without directing students in any particular way or towards a specific conclusion... I think this is a better model for critical thought and political discourse than something like traditional debate because it encourages students to look to facts and moral considerations without the constraints a foregone or pre-determined conclusion creates.

Rylee Walker, University of Montana graduate student instructor and former Whitworth University IEB team member, echoes much of the same.

> Problems are often best solved when common ground can be reached, and Ethics Bowl welcomes common ground in a way debate does not... I am forever grateful for the ways in which Ethics Bowl helped me grow my confidence, my ability to identify and to foreground ethics in decision-making, and my skills in presenting persuasive ideas as a structured discussion instead of just a structured argument.

Claire Howe, Oregon HSEB judge and Executive Director of The Raven Corps, a youth-centered anti-oppression group based in Portland, Oregon, shared her enthusiasm for the same reasons.

> The whole concept of pinning down the most ethical argument, in a supportive atmosphere, instead of intentionally creating confrontation… makes so much sense!

While debate suggests black-and-white simplicity, moral equivalence, and that issues are settled by reciting a preselected script, Ethics Olympiad judge and coach from Adelaide University in Australia, Tim Nailer, explains how Ethics Bowl demonstrates the necessity of collaboration while celebrating nuance and depth.

> Rather than simply presenting a case and leaving it at that, [Ethics Bowl] requires students to respond to counterexamples from their peers and from expert judges. In doing so, students move beyond the obvious to consider the complexity and the subtlety of issues in question and learn to resist the competing pitfalls of "the answer is easy" and "all answers are equally correct."

Debate does indeed court the extremes of relativism and absolutism. And debate's pressure to prove the position a team's been arbitrarily assigned as unquestionably correct encourages a disingenuous mercenaryism where "winning" overrides truth. This difference was appreciated quickly by Houston high schooler Benjamin Who, who was inspired to found a team at his school.

> I realized that the winner in a debate round is the person who can "outsmart" their opponent, often by misrepresenting or misconstruing evidence or using logical tricks. When I discovered Ethics Bowl, I was fascinated by its emphasis on finding the truth.

With a nod to difficult epistemological questions surrounding the nature of moral claims, Northern California High School Ethics Bowl organizer Kyle Robertson of UC Santa Cruz says much of the same in *The Ethics Bowl Way*.

> Put simply, Ethics Bowl is a formal argument format that refuses to put the goal of persuasion above the goal of truth, or at least the honest pursuit of a better answer.[19]

Ethics Bowl provides a character-expanding venue where participants can risk being wrong without embarrassment, or at least without as much embarrassment as usual. Already quoted above, Vegas attorney and former Intercollegiate Bowler Francesca Hovagimian argues that the benefits don't only apply to social harmony, but interpersonal relationships as well.

> I think traditional debate promotes harmful forms of motivated reasoning as well as polarization in its participants and those viewing it, and very little is

[19] Page 12.

> actually achieved in terms of compromise or reconsideration… if anything, people become more entrenched in their positions. Ethics Bowl allows the participants to reach middle ground and understanding without "losing face," and I think as a result real progress is more likely to be made using the Ethics Bowl model.

One factor possibly in Ethics Bowl's favor is that it may be more appealing to younger generations. Many Boomers and Xers may be content to battle issues out. But high schooler Benjamin Who in Houston suggests that Gen Z and beyond may find Ethics Bowl's style more consistent with their desires and priorities.

> I personally know many friends who are interested in how debate trains logical thinking, public speaking, and evidence analysis, but are turned off by its combative nature. They want to learn how to discuss big ideas with others without having to confront and fight their opponents. Ethics Bowl is the perfect solution—it maintains a fun, competitive atmosphere while allowing participants to focus on learning and pursuing the advance of knowledge.

This was echoed by an anonymous Ethics Olympiad coach in New Zealand who was pleasantly surprised that it wasn't nearly as debatey as they had expected.

> From the material provided, I expected the set up to be more like formal debating, which I think put some of my students off. Now that I know what it's like, I think it will be easier to recruit students.

Archie Stapleton, longtime Ethics Olympiad coach, judge, moderator, and trainer, founder of the Modes Ponens Institute, and organizer of the Pan-American Ethics Olympiad, captures the contrast well. And he's in a better position to do it than most given his roots in traditional debate.

> I think there is an understanding that competitive debate has its limitations. It is too adversarial, and produces students who can be needlessly argumentative, and think a conversation is successful only insofar as their "opponent" has been "defeated" (I only say this because I was one of them). The structure of the Olympiad creates a different sort of thinking: still analytic, careful, and structured, but also constructive and productive. When team B questions team A, they get to offer suggestions that genuinely help team A think about the topic, which has been a significant part of the competition's success.

Canadian High School Ethics Bowl co-organizer Nick Tanchuk shares Stapleton's assessment.

> I think the thing that is most promising about Ethics Bowl is its non-adversarial, fallibilist approach to inquiry into practical questions. Where other similar activities, such as debate, can be quite adversarial in their structure, Ethics Bowl cultivates a different set of virtues by its collaborative, evidence responsive, dialectical design.

Ethics Bowl's "non-adversarial" and "fallibilist" approach—so well put. Portland State HSEB judge Ted Kaye offers an equally eloquent unofficial motto.

> The "non-competitive competition" aspect creates a positive tension and an unusual opportunity to learn how the world works, contrary to the "winner take all" ethos of a debate.

Former debate coach, communication ethics professor, and Intercollegiate Ethics Bowl-winning coach, Mike Ingram, argues that Ethics Bowl's insistence that teams acknowledge and honorably engage a hypothetical objector is one of its highest benefits. For charitably representing and responding to views we don't endorse is rare, yet uniquely instructive.

> This has many implications. It can foster a sense of intellectual honesty by identifying places where another viewpoint has something important to say, and students must represent that view in a fair fashion. That also causes teams to assess the strengths and limitations of the claims they make. It can foster respect for other views and those who hold them by requiring a complete explanation of them, and not just a casual dismissal in passing. The requirement of considering alternate ways of thinking helps foster this important skill for life beyond the Bowl.

With Ethics Bowl enjoying so many comparative advantages, can a reasonable case in favor of traditional debate be made?

## It Can't Be All Bad...

I've had debate apologists argue that since teams don't know which position they'll be assigned on competition day, they're forced to study the weaknesses and advantages of all perspectives, and in the process develop a deeper understanding of important issues. A more informed citizenry is a good thing, and outside of the competition, debaters are free to decide for themselves which positions are best.

While this is true, Ethics Bowl delivers similar benefits without debate's drawbacks. For one, rather than encouraging defensive groupthink, Ethics Bowl explicitly requires self-critique. The expectation that teams will proactively respond to a reasonable objection, which IEB coach Mike Ingram found so valuable, is right there on the judges' score sheet in item 1.c.

> Did the team's presentation indicate both awareness and thoughtful consideration of different viewpoints, including those that would loom large in the reasoning of individuals who disagree with the team's position?

Debate does require teams to examine issues from multiple angles. But preparing to aggressively defend whatever stance you're randomly assigned reinforces an unprincipled ambivalence educators have no business encouraging. In other words, while debaters may expand their understanding, it's warped by the knowledge that the view they'll defend at the competition won't turn on their rational assessment, but on the flip of a coin. The result is alumni great at defending whatever they're told to believe, but untrained in deciding what's worth believing.

Attorney Francesca Hovagimian, whom we quoted above, published a New York Times op-ed with UC Santa Cruz philosophy professor Jonathan Ellis on this point when she was still in law school in 2019.

> Debate discourages the kind of listening and reasoning that is critical to a healthy democracy. Student debaters don't deliberate about what they themselves believe or should believe. They don't cultivate the disposition to listen to others with the real possibility of changing their minds. On the contrary, they practice listening with eagle ears for opposing points to pounce on. Rather than increasing their comfort with being wrong, they can deepen an attitude of certainty. School debate doesn't have to be this way, though. In fact, many schools around the country are gravitating to alternative forms of debate that set the goals of truth and understanding over the goal of persuasion. A good example is the Ethics Bowl.[20]

Ethics Bowl not only asks participants to think freely and to take responsibility for their conclusions (which students absolutely love, by the way), but teaches them how. Teams spend weeks parsing case details (more on those cool cases in chapter 5: The Cases!), contrasting shared and conflicting moral intuitions, deciding together which factors are most relevant, which moral frameworks apply most powerfully, and how to best balance all the reasons and ideas in play.

20 "Are School Debate Competitions Bad for Our Political Discourse?", Oct 12, 2019.

This isn't a theoretical exercise where participants can comfortably guard what they believe in their heart of hearts. Rather, it requires exposing our true beliefs, knowing full well we'll be scrutinized and judged. Rather than, "One way a person *could* argue is..." it's "I really think the right thing to do is..." Ethics Bowl requires an intellectual and emotional ownership that inspires courage and builds character.

Unanimity is rare, so if you see a team member squirm while another is speaking, the cause is probably lingering disagreement. But requiring teams to decide the cases pushes participants to accept responsibility for their views—to be able to logically defend them not only to themselves, but to their coach and team members, in anticipation of pushback come Bowl day. They know the other team will be cordial, but unsympathetic. And so rather than burying doubts, as members of an insulated tribe might, they have good reason to admit and work through them together, even when that means modifying their initial view.

Debate prep, on the other hand, does encourage thorough research and multi-angle issue analysis. But it doesn't require teams to take a stand. This fosters a cold, irresponsible detachment, suggesting that the position a person chooses is more a matter of appeasing an authority than enlightened conviction.

## Common Ground

If you've been or are currently a debater, know that my goal hasn't been to gloat or belittle. My beef is with the format, not the people. I know the debate community's intentions are and always have been pure.

For example, The American Debate League lists on its website the goals of improving students' critical thinking skill, helping them overcome public speaking fear, cultivating leadership and creativity—even preparing at-risk students for the realities of a competitive and sometimes hostile world.[21] There's no denying the fact that debate helps young people find their voice, gives them confidence, and readies them for personal and professional success.

Debaters are goodhearted volunteers investing countless hours in what's been the default way to bolster citizen advocacy for as long as anyone can remember. Debate's purpose is to empower the weak and embolden the marginalized. Who could argue with that?

Also, perhaps debate is kinder than I've given it credit. I'm harsh on the effects of coin-flip positioning. But randomly assigning sides rather than requiring teams to decide and defend one could be an act of conflict avoidance, decreasing pre-debate drama and compassionately insulating participants from personal attack. It could also be motivated by humility, acknowledgement that moral and

[21] "Benefits of Debate," americandebateleague.org/benefits-of-debate.html

political issues are super tough, and so the best non-experts can hope to do is play an advocacy role for one side or the other and see how the conversation progresses. There's no reason to assume the debate community's intentions are anything but honorable.

In fact, some debaters explicitly share Ethics Bowl's goals and values. For example, in response to Hovagimian and Ellis's op-ed critique of debate quoted above, University of Texas business ethics professor Robert Prentice penned a rejoinder for UT's *Ethics Unwrapped* blog that touted debate's ability to help participants transcend affirming biases and evaluate arguments objectively.

> Debaters, more than others, know that there are at least two sides to every argument because they've practiced arguing for both sides. They know better than others that they should be open minded…
>
> Because of their training, debaters also know better than most that some arguments are better than others, that real facts should be more persuasive than "alternative facts," and that calling something "fake news" just because you wish it were fake news does not make it fake news.
>
> Those of us who wish to be moral actors must realize that (a) in the political arena, we must fight against the undue impact of the self-serving bias, and (b) that self-serving bias undermines the integrity of our

> moral judgments just as it does our political judgments.[22]

Further, consider this call for debate reform presented by Clea Conner, Chief Executive Officer of the Open to Debate Foundation. Presented at the World Economic Forum's annual meeting in Davos in 2024, Conner makes a powerful case that seems very much aligned with Ethics Bowl's benefits and mission.[23]

> We are living in an era of historic, unprecedented levels of political polarization and partisan division. "The truth" can't be trusted. "The facts" are selectively presented… Public policy conversations have devolved into the exchange of quippy sound-bites, not the exchange of substantive ideas. We too often see unhinged meandering shouting matches with little moderation, creating battlegrounds where only the loudest voices prevail.

Agreed. Her proposed solution? A rehabilitation of debate's role and purpose that sounds an awful lot like an ad for Ethics Bowl.

[22] "Debating Debate," October 17, 2019.
[23] "In Our Polarized World, Debate Has Never Been So Important," 14 January 2024.

> Debate offers a unique platform for building empathy. It necessitates that participants not only articulate their viewpoints but also listen to and engage with opposing arguments… Winning should not be about overpowering your opponent with rhetoric, but about bridging the gap of understanding between disparate viewpoints. Imagine a format that values reflective pauses and encourages participants to genuinely consider the perspectives of their counterparts.

Can I imagine such a format? Yes! I suppose traditional debate could do these things. And I want it to do these things. I'm just not convinced it can do these things nearly as well as Ethics Bowl. However, the shared interest in building empathy, enriching understanding, and earnest listening is very, very welcome. Conner continues.

> This isn't about diluting the rigor of arguments; it's about enriching them with a dimension of human empathy that's often missing in our polarized discourse. The true measure of a successful debate should be the extent to which it fosters mutual understanding and opens avenues for continued dialogue. The goal is to emerge not with a winner and a loser, but with a richer, more nuanced appreciation for complex issues and solutions.

Connor goes on to call for the inclusion of more interpersonal issues, which Ethics Bowl does, to foster a welcoming, respectful public discourse, which Ethics Bowl does, and to encourage high standards when it comes to scrutinizing empirical claims. This last area hasn't been Ethics Bowl's strength, but Ethics Bowl advocate, Fort Lewis College philosophy professor, and author of *Beyond Fake News: Finding the Truth in a World of Misinformation,* Justin McBrayer, does offer an improvement strategy we'll consider in chapter 9: Ethics Bowl's Future. But Conner's closing line suggests debate leaders may be ready and eager to pivot.

> This [very much Ethics Bowl-sounding] approach might just be the key to addressing the polarization and distrust that is eroding the fabric of our global society.

As we established in the opening chapter, Ethics Bowlers aren't pompous know-it-alls scowling down their noses. Well, a few could be… But not the vast majority, and not anyone featured in this book.

But if you've been at all convinced that traditional debate might have room for improvement, and if you agree with Open to Debate CEO Clea Conner that the time for reform is now, let's combine forces.

Google Intercollegiate Ethics Bowl or National High School Ethics Bowl or National Middle School Ethics Bowl or Ethics Olympiad or Ethics Bowl Canada or Ethics Bowl China or Ethics Cup. Poke around at EthicsBowl.org. If you're not sure what to do next, send your questions to matt@mattdeaton.com. Someone will gladly connect you with your closest organizer, share a current case set, a score sheet, and judging rubric, as well as coaching resources including written guides, videos, and in some cases invites to live trainings. If you already know Ethics Bowl and are willing to help welcome newcomers, email and I'll add you to my debate conversion support network.

A volunteer may be willing to help re-train your debate team or recruit a new Ethics Bowl group. To do a test drive on your own schedule, look up "Ethics Bowl for the Classroom," a free, simple guide on how to run a basic Bowl in-house.

If you hate it, nothing lost. But if you love it, the barriers to conversion are very, very low. If you're already familiar with debate, and especially if you already have a team, join us. But first, let's get a better idea of why these Ethics Bowl characters are so gung ho.

# CHAPTER 4

# WHY THEY DO IT

Ethics Bowl positions are almost always unpaid. A few include a modest stipend or honorarium. But the number of salaried Ethics Bowl posts is dwarfed by an army of dedicated volunteers.

I asked those walking the walk why they do it. While reasons vary, there are themes. Perhaps someone's *why* will inspire you.

## Judges

Let's begin with one of our most important and difficult roles—judging. It may look easy from the outside. But anyone who's done it understands the pressures and perils, and the precision required to foster excellence without crushing egos.

Push too hard during the judge Q&A period, and you risk discouraging new teams. But go too easy, and you risk leaving them wondering why they invested all those hours preparing. Balancing high standards with encouragement requires intention and care.

Quality judging also requires self-awareness and attention to how you're apt to be perceived. Fail to maintain objectivity in both substance and appearance, and risk undermining trust. And once you've lost a coach's, a participant's, or a parent's trust, it's tough to regain.

For better or worse, judges are also ambassadors for academic philosophy. When I judge, I'll often reassure new teams that the most nervous person at an Ethics Bowl is a judge. We may look calm. But who's under more pressure to say something smart? Judges can affirm that moral reasoning is indeed a learnable skill, and that the love of wisdom is worthy of students' time and tuition. Or we can add doubt to the humanities' already beleaguered status.

In other words, judges are the true face of Ethics Bowl. Organizers can talk about attitude shifts and the virtues of civility all day. But as our exemplars on the frontlines, if our judges aren't patient, wise, and kind, then all those platitudes will feel hollow.

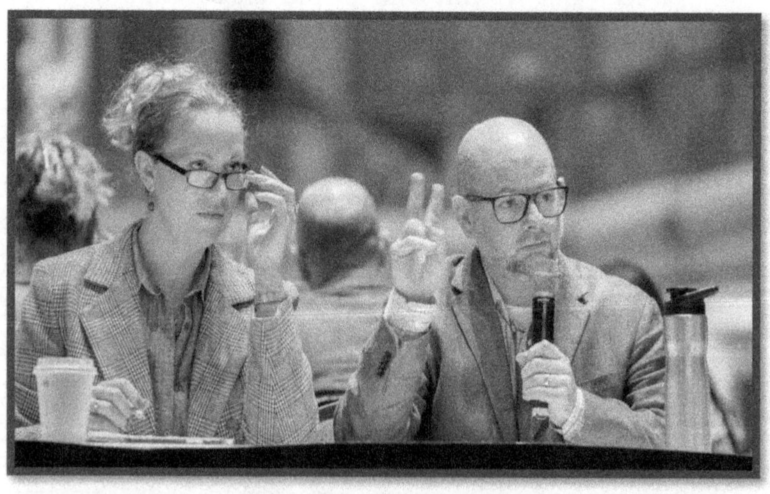

DEBORAH MOWER AND JOHN GARCIA JUDGING AT THE IEB NATIONALS IN 2024 *COURTESY OF APPE IEB®*

In addition to the pressure of representing both philosophy and Ethics Bowl, judging is time consuming, mentally taxing, and emotionally draining. Maybe I'm overly sensitive. But I've said no to judging opportunities far more often than I care to admit, not because I don't love and believe in Ethics Bowl, but because deciding a winner is my least favorite part. When the teams are equally prepared, thoughtful, and respectful, when they're modeling the maturity Ethics Bowl wants, and when you can tell hearts will be broken, choosing which team is best can feel like an unjust chore.

I'm sure others feel the same. (I'm not the best judge recruiter, I know.) Yet hundreds continue to answer the call. Why? Most of the time, like other Ethics Bowl enthusiasts, judges believe in the mission.

Many are dissatisfied with the sad state of public discourse. They realize how embarrassingly tribal our political culture has become. And rather than recoiling or scoffing, they've decided to be part of a solution.

This has been the case for Australian Ethics Olympiad judge Dirk Baltzy, whose *why* includes how much better suited Ethics Bowl is than traditional debate at cultivating engaged citizens.

> One of the things I like best about the way Ethics Olympiad is set up is the fact that it is precisely NOT debating. Since teams are encouraged to acknowledge good arguments and to contribute

> collaboratively to the resolution of the question, the activity embodies the value of truth-seeking—not sophistic defense of a position that you yourself might not think is true. To their credit, I think the student-participants really get this. At a time when civil discourse in so many places has become so acrimonious, this is an important value for young people to absorb. In my limited experience, many of them are truly better in this regard than the so-called grown-ups in our societies.

Andrew Costantino, also of Australia's Ethics Olympiad, has been a judge, a coach, an organizer, and trainer. He confirms that the need for calm, reasoned deliberation is universal, and that this is a motivator for him as well.

> Moral discourse is often partisan and polarized, the Ethics Olympiad rewards open discussion, capacity to change your mind, nuance and flexibility. It promotes empathy, critical reflection, and respectful dialogue. All of these things have the potential to enhance the character of participants and encourage thoughtful and reflective engagement in the world.

It's the promise of rejuvenating public discourse that convinces so many judges to sacrifice their time and volunteer their expertise. And when they see it working—

when they witness students behaving better than many so-called grown-ups—it's easier for them to make those wrenching winner vs. loser decisions round after round. Most do it with a warm regality that conveys the community's gratitude to coaches, participants, and their families for joining us in being part of a solution. One example: the Oregon HSEB's Ted Kaye.

> I make a point to come in a suit—as dressed up as some of them [the participants], shake hands with each one after the match, and model appropriate adult behavior. I always provide specific extra feedback on the evaluation forms.

Quality, committed, repeat-volunteer judges like Ted do not go unnoticed. The Oregon Bowl's organizer, Dave Weber, shared his deep appreciation, and how Ted consistently conveys his admiration for all participants regardless of a team's ultimate placing.

> It's great to see [Ted] sitting with the competitors at lunch (he's done judging by then) and chatting them up, and demonstrating a real, adult's interest in these kids' opinions.

Judges like Ted, Dirk, and Andrew can be found giving teams their positive attention weekends during Bowl season not only across the country, but around the world. It takes courage and personal accountability to judge, for you're exposing yourself to critique, and under pressure to uphold the dignified image and high standards of philosophy and Ethics Bowl. Their role is appreciated by those who understand the sacrifice, but overlooked by most. So, the next time you're at a Bowl, take a moment to thank a judge. They definitely deserve it. Just wait until after final scores are in so they know you're being sincere rather than sucking up.

## Coaches

While judging ain't easy, compared to one group, it's a cushy gig. Sure, judges have to decide a winner, they're under pressure to prove their expertise, and in many places they're the face of both Ethics Bowl and academic philosophy. But their time commitment is manageable, they get first dibs on pastries, and on Bowl day especially, people do tend to kiss their ass.

The backbone of Ethics Bowl, the volunteers in the trenches, day in, day out, the mentors recruiting, molding and in some cases putting up with the youthful drama of the new and improved generation, the people responsible for organizing practices, navigating sign-ups, taking care of payments and untold travel logistics most never see, are Ethics Bowl's true heroes, our coaches.

A high school or middle school Ethics Bowl coach's specialty may be English, History, Government, Speech—pretty much anything. Where I come from, that's welcome and completely fine. Philosophy is rarely taught before college, especially in public schools. And so anyone with the interest is very much invited to coach.

The dearth of pre-college philosophy instruction is one reason Ethics Bowl is so valuable. It can be a catalyst for the creation of philosophy clubs,[24] drive demand for new elective philosophy classes, or simply inspire a student's independent study. Coaches are sometimes philosophy teachers, but usually only in private schools, and this is more the exception than the rule in high school and below.

On the collegiate level, and also the high school level, some Ethics Bowl coaches are debate coaches looking to boost their teams' seriousness, or to simply keep them sharp during the off season. However, most college Ethics Bowl coaches are ethics professors.

Sometimes an Intercollegiate Ethics Bowl coach will also serve as a High School Ethics Bowl organizer, recruiting their IEB team to assist coach, moderate, and judge. And sometimes folks will go full SuperSocrates and decide to do it all. For example, Weber State philosophy professor Richard Greene in Utah has coached both Intercollegiate and Bioethics Bowl teams. But he also co-founded and continues to run the Wasatch Regional IEB. He launched and continues to help organize the IEB Summer Ethics Bowl Workshop—

[24] See high school coach Andersen's excellent 2023 article, "Linking Ethics Bowl Cases to Philosophy Club Topics" at ethicsbowl.org/2023/04/19/linking-ethics-bowl-cases-to-philosophy-club-topics-guide/

an annual Zoom-based homecoming, strategy session, and morale boost open to all Ethics Bowl enthusiasts and free to attend. In fact, over the years Richard has served in nearly every imaginable Ethics Bowl role, including rules committee chair, board member, national championship organizer—even IEB director. He even organizes Ethics Slams and Ethics Bowls in prisons.

There are a surprising number of Ethics Bowl superhumans just as committed and involved as Richard. You know who you are. Thank you! However, their example is inspiring, but extreme. Should *you* find this Ethics Bowl thing worthwhile, feel free to pick one role and do it well.

THE 2025 IEB NATIONAL CHAMPIONS FROM MACALESTER COLLEGE OF SAINT PAUL, MINNESOTA *COURTESY OF APPE IEB®*

For example, Michael Andersen, philosophy club advisor and Ethics Bowl coach at Vancouver School of Arts and Academics in Washington state, is one of the best in the nation. His *why* is largely Ethics Bowl's ability to temper arrogance, as well as its insistence that participants imagine how a reasonable person might disagree with them. Humble, respectful, curious engagement may seem basic. But it's far too uncommon, and a big reason coaches like Andersen get and stay involved.

> This element of education is often woefully deficient or missing entirely from humanities instruction at the middle and high school levels in many American public schools. Indeed, too often we see a lack of these civic virtues (charitable consideration of differing views, intellectual integrity) in our American public discourse among adults. I viewed (and still view) Ethics Bowl as an attempt to counter this dangerous cultural trend.

Andersen went on to tie these benefits back to their impact on politics.

> American citizens in general sorely need more philosophical training, but particularly the variety of informed, rational civic engagement that encourages careful listening and nuanced thinking. Witnessing students develop their critical thinking skills and

> linguistic fluency through Ethics Bowl case analysis and discussion with other teams excites and inspires me, as a volunteer coach, as much as it does them.

Andersen also shared his love for how Ethics Bowl is practical and directly practiced. The community doesn't preach an ideal in a vacuum, but helps participants tackle some of our toughest and most timely topics head on. While teams rarely arrive at a complete consensus, they almost always learn and grow. In the process, defenses come down, mutual appreciation goes up, and everyone can see how almost no position earnestly held is truly baseless. As shared by coach Andersen:

> The best part about Ethics Bowl is the opportunity for students to develop topical and cultural awareness through exposure to real-world issues. Equally significant is the realization among our students that people outside of their immediate circle of influence can be intelligent, thoughtful, and decent—while also arguing opposing views than the students' own. Such experiences tend to broaden their intellectual horizons and refine their moral intuitions. This also tends to promote the kind of respectful coexistence necessary for civil society.

Indeed, with political violence worsening, helping participants realize that "people outside of their immediate circle of influence can be intelligent, thoughtful, and decent" is becoming increasingly important. IEB-winning coach Mike Ingram at Whitworth University understands Ethics Bowl's transformational power better than most. He's been coaching since 2003 and has watched students blossom time and again. But it wasn't until recent political tensions that he fully appreciated how Ethics Bowl uniquely addresses this critical need.

> The past two presidential elections in the United States have been marked by sharp partisan rhetoric often including vilification of those who hold differing views. I firmly believe the presence of opposing viewpoints by Team one in the Bowl helps students develop both an ability and disposition to look at the views of others in honest and charitable terms. This work helps prepare them to be good citizens in our society. Perhaps it equips them to help others reap this key benefit of the Bowl, to look at others and their ideas in a new and honest light, even in disagreement.

With algorithms, partisan media outlets, and opportunists driving us apart, the world *needs* activities that help us interpret our neighbors charitably, to view them "and their ideas in a new and honest light, even in disagreement." And while Ingram was inspired to say this by the acrimony of recent presidential elections, he actually wrote these words before the January 6th riots at the U.S.

Capitol in 2021, before the 2024 assassination attempts on then-candidate Donald Trump, before the assassination of Minnesota state representative Melissa Horman and activist Charlie Kirk in 2025, and before whatever other awful things have happened by the time you're reading these words.

Ethics Bowl won't end political violence. But it's reasonable to expect more and worse political violence without serious, substantive intervention. Ethics Bowl *can* raise expectations and lower tensions. It can teach our youth to listen to those who disagree with them, to give them the benefit of the doubt, and to recognize our shared imperfect humanity, subject to similar pressures and limitations, driven by similar needs and fears. As Superman said in the 2025 movie, beneath our costumes, we're essential the same.[25]

> I love. I get scared. I wake up every morning and despite not knowing what to do, I put one foot in front of the other and I try to make the best choices I can. I screw up all the time. But that's being human.

As Lex Luthor relishes pointing out, Superman, with his Kryptonian DNA, isn't technically a member of the biological category Homo sapiens. But he is a member of the moral category persons. Ethics Bowl discussions are a calming reminder that dividing labels like left, right,

[25] With SuperSocrates on the cover, you knew Superman had to be in here somewhere.

Democrat, Republican, Earthling, Kryptonian are ultimately superficial. Underneath, we're all people, and it's harder to convince us to hate or harm one another when we can see ourselves in would-be targets. At a time when so many forces are busy demonizing, Ethics Bowl is one of the few busy humanizing.

Ethics Bowl also combats political violence by sharpening reasoning skill, for militant radicalism has a tough time thriving in the presence of clear thinking. Hubris is understandable when you're exposed to a single perspective being actively sheltered from critique. But nonsense tends to become apparent when subjected to the power of logic. I'm biased, but agree with Ethics Olympiad coach Tim Nailer when he argues that simply doing philosophy makes us more reasonable, mature, and impervious to indoctrination.

> Through philosophy, one learns the importance of listening to opposing viewpoints and to neither uncritically accept or reject these views, either in whole or in part. Philosophy helps people distinguish good reasons from bad ones, and creates a disposition to be more consistent and less dogmatic. All else being equal, if an activity helps people develop these skills and dispositions, then it's an activity worth supporting. This is true of philosophy in general and Ethics Olympiads in particular.

Nailer may not have experienced the same degree of vitriol and divisiveness in Australia that's becoming commonplace in the U.S. But he still appreciates our shared need for earnest critical thinking, self-evaluation, and principled consistency in our views. These are indeed dispositions philosophy cultivates generally. And Ethics Bowl just happens to be an especially practical, especially accessible, and especially fun way to do it. However, that doesn't mean the growth that Ethics Bowl promises comes easy.

For example, highly decorated retired Army colonel and University of Florida IEB coach, Brian Ray, likens his ethics classes and Ethics Bowl prep to a gym. And just like the physical gym, the ethics gym requires effort to see results. No one improves their 40-yard dash by walking. No one bests their squat max by skipping leg day. And no one gets better at moral decision-making by sheltering within their emotional comfort zone.

> I tell students, this is not a classroom—this is the ethics gym. And if you want to feel comfortable, then just drop the class…
>
> Nobody goes to the gym to sit on the couch. You go to the gym to work out, lift weights, and get stronger and better… This is not a safe space here. This is called ethics gym.

> And if you want a safe space, leave the class. If you want to get better at making hard, difficult decisions, then get ready.
>
> We're all going to work out, and your teammates are going to spot you. We're all here to make each other stronger and better.[26]

While I love the gym analogy and even more the "teammate spotter" connection, Ray may come across as a bit *too* gung ho. I'll acknowledge in chapter 13: Make It Mandatory? how ethical discussions can be extremely personal, sometimes feeling like a threat to our very identity. Cultivating an atmosphere where those discussions are possible requires earning a great deal of mutual trust. But as an Air Force vet, I can appreciate Ray's tough-love Army enthusiasm, and if you watch the "How to Use Ethics Bowl in the Classroom" video from which this quote was taken, you'll feel the warmth in his demeanor. Coach Ray is animated, but caring, as you'd expect from anyone involved with Ethics Bowl, retired Army colonel or not. And his emphasis that students have one another's backs ("your teammates are going to spot you") confirms that he fully appreciates the stakes, and knows how to push students

26 "How to Use Ethics Bowl in the Classroom," from the 2023 Ethics Bowl Workshop hosted by IEB and the Association for Practical and Professional Ethics, posted July 20, 2023, 54-minute mark at YouTube.com/watch ?v=YFSXyQfQIBI

without breaking them, ensuring ethics gym enables growth without injury.

Ray goes on to say that while being up front that ethics class is not a safe space can be jarring at first, the same students who are shy and reserved the first week are usually great friends by week four or five. Also, remember that he's working with college students, where it's acceptable to be a bit more direct. But rest assured ethics teachers and Ethics Bowl coaches are sensitive to their students' needs. Army colonel or not, I'm sure Ray's a teddy bear when the situation calls for it. Because if our coaches lacked the emotional intelligence and tact necessary to navigate the difficult topics we cover, our participants wouldn't love it so much.

## Participants

Sometimes Ethics Bowlers are recruited by a charismatic teacher. If you already enjoy Mr. McConkey's class,[27] he asks nicely and convinces you that you'd be good at it, it's easy to say yes. Bribery also doesn't hurt. IEB coach Greg Wright at Snow College in Utah has had success enticing students with pizza, though he's found it's best to delay the feast until a few weeks in. (Wright reported an Ethics Bowl interest pizza party drawing 35 students, but

[27] Dr. Lance McConkey was the History and Contemporary Issues teacher at Sequoyah High School serving students in Vonore and Madisonville, Tennessee, credited with bringing Ethics Bowl to my hometown, and affording me the honor of assist coaching close to home. Thank you and happy retirement, Lance!

when actual practice started a week later, only 1 returned.) But from my experience visiting schools and speaking to high school students in particular, oftentimes it's not so much the person pitching it or the pizza promised as the style of inquiry.

Oh, the looks of suspicion and disbelief when students used to memorizing uncontestable facts are asked, "Well, what do *you* think?" and then an adult actually listens! Yet more shock when that adult summarizes their points on the board, helps them consider counterpoints, recognize and repair weak arguments, and work together to sketch a tentative view they can jointly endorse.

This is a welcome surprise in an environment that so often prioritizes compliance and efficiency. Teachers are tasked with covering an overwhelmingly dense curriculum and evaluated based on students' performance of defined skills and retention of provided facts. When your effectiveness as a professional is judged in terms of multiple guess test scores, open-ended discussions can seem a waste. And with a diverse student population with a variety of personalities, limitations, and needs, it's understandable that education often amounts to the memorization and regurgitation of settled knowledge.

Ah, but not every subject is as straightforward as Biology or Algebra, and students naturally crave organic idea exploration. Consider the experience of Rylee Walker, University of Montana grad student and former IEB competitor at Whitworth University.

> I am forever grateful for the ways in which Ethics Bowl helped me grow my confidence, my ability to identify and to foreground ethics in decision-making, and my skills in presenting persuasive ideas as a structured discussion.

Rylee also loved how Ethics Bowl taught her how to disagree gracefully, and how earnest discussion opens us to friendship in ways little else can.

> Ethics Bowl prioritizes understanding the other team's arguments and agreeing where possible. This humanizes the arguments, and it also allows ideas to build off of each other to support the best possible answer to the question… There is nothing quite like huddling up as a group after the question is announced to devise a quick plan of action. To me, Ethics Bowl really symbolizes the idea of being "better together."

This friend-making benefit wasn't something I expected when soliciting interviewees. However, many of the people I admire and respect most, I've met through Ethics Bowl. So it shouldn't have come as a surprise that participants would highlight deep friendships as a key benefit. DePauw University IEB National Champion captain Marko Mavrovic confirmed that Ethics Bowl is an unexpectedly excellent forum for developing ties that bind.

> People who normally do not mingle are brought together in a space in which nothing else matters but the quality of their arguments and the sharpness of their critiques. Peers who I had known in other capacities, I grew to know (and respect) more through Ethics Bowl. Some of the most important friendships of my life started in Ethics Bowl practice.

Since we're supposed to be changing the world rather than matchmaking BFFs, "make friends!" isn't a recruitment slogan I've ever considered using. But maybe we should all start.

Just as the relational benefits should have been obvious, it shouldn't be surprising that participants' reasons for valuing Ethics Bowl shift as they age and are better able to put the experience into context. For example, Francesca Hovagimian joined Ethics Bowl on a graduate teaching assistant's recommendation while studying at the University of California Santa Cruz. Reflecting today as a practicing attorney, she can more clearly see its initial appeal, as well as how it's shaped her life path.

> I think the biggest draw for me was the chance to discuss and think about ethical hypotheticals. Maybe that sounds boring, but I really enjoyed digging into moral dilemmas with my classmates and eventually forming positions for the competition.

Indeed, many people long for the chance to think through moral questions in a respectful, methodical, cooperative way. Maybe Francesca didn't consciously know she was looking for that engagement at the time. But with the perspective of age and experience, she now understands how Ethics Bowl satisfied that latent human need. Today she values more than ever its invitation to let go of what we're supposed to think, and to simply think.

> I continue to support Ethics Bowl because I think it provides a great opportunity for students to actually consider the moral dimensions of issues without being constrained by any particular ideological position or pre-determined conclusion, and because it promotes critical thinking AND productive discussion.

And as an attorney, Francesca can see how well Ethics Bowl set her up for academic and professional success.

> As an aside, I also think Ethics Bowl prepared me extremely well for law school and lawyering! I gained skills in logical reasoning, public speaking, and improvisation that I didn't get from any other courses during my undergrad career… Ultimately, I would like to see Ethics Bowl replace traditional debate in both high school and collegiate venues.

While Francesca was especially intrigued by Ethics Bowl's focus on moral questions, some participants are interested in philosophy generally and see Ethics Bowl simply as a way to get more of it. For example, Houston high schooler Benjamin Who, like most public school students in the U.S., likely wouldn't otherwise have direct access to trained philosophers but for Ethics Bowl.

> Getting feedback from experts, who are often philosophy Ph.D. students or professors, allows us to learn from the best and develop our skills under the best mentorship.

Benjamin is too kind. If only the philosophy grad students who volunteer as assistant coaches, judges, and moderators knew how much they were appreciated! But let there be no doubt that Ethics Bowl is successful and growing because participants like Francesca and Benjamin simply love it.

Mary Helen Wade, co-founder of the South Carolina HSEB, confirmed our participants' enthusiasm with her own account of five-star customer satisfaction.

> As several students shared with me over the past couple of years, Ethics Bowl was their favorite activity. One told me she wanted to redo her senior year so she could participate in Ethics Bowl again.

Repeat your senior year? Just to do another season of Ethics Bowl? I'm not sure anything could have persuaded me to stick around for another year of high school. But that's exactly how much many of our participants love it, which Canadian High School Ethics Bowl co-organizer Estelle Lamoureux reports as well.

> Former students have clearly stated that the Ethics Bowl was the very best experience they had in high school. They discover that the truth is sometimes elusive, hidden amongst the misspoken half-truths and outright fabrications. The beauty of the Ethics Bowl is we are teaching students "how to think, not what to think" without diminishing creative thought.

The fact that Ethics Bowl respects well-reasoned perspectives, rather than demanding positions align with a predetermined ideology ("*how* to think, not *what* to think"), is a big reason people join and return. The freedom to follow good reasons wherever they lead—left, right, in a corkscrew through economics, biology, metaphysics, and back—is of course the way humans naturally think. The Ethics Bowl experience exposes just how distorting two-party thought boxes are, and how much progress we can make when untethered from their typical us vs. them expectations.

We'll talk more about the neutrality the Ethics Bowl community works hard to maintain in a later chapter. But first, while judges are our ambassadors, coaches our workhorses, and participants our future, let's talk about the behind-the-scenes wizards who make it all happen.

## Organizers

Ethics Bowl would not be possible but for a dedicated group of selfless saints sacrificing their time, sleep, and peace of mind for the cause. Organizing tests your project management skill—not a trait for which philosophers are typically known—your persuasiveness, your perseverance, and in some cases your friendships and sanity. It's also fun and rewarding, and may be the best way many can use their unique expertise to better the world. But while you should thank the next Ethics Bowl judge you meet and shake a coach's hand, the next time you see an organizer, please give them a hug. Ask permission first. But they probably need it!

Yet, you'll rarely hear them complain, and the way they fit organizing into their busy lives and cope with the demands is probably as varied as their paths to Ethics Bowl. For example, University of Findlay philosophy professor Matt Stolick was introduced by a colleague who invited him to judge an IEB in 2009. Impressed by the teams' ability to reason without computers, phones, or notes, and to do so with such class and authenticity, Stolick thought to himself:

> I would be happy if students who took one of my ethics courses were able to do what these Ethics Bowl students just did. I was converted.

ETHICS BOWL ORGANIZING ALL-STARS, RICHARD GREENE, RACHEL ROBISON-GREENE, DEBORAH MOWER, AND ALEX RICHARDSON AT THE 2025 IEB NATIONALS *COURTESY OF APPE IEB®*

Now in his eleventh year as the organizer of the Ohio HSEB and his third year as Findlay IEB team coach, Stolick worries how Americans in particular are increasingly self-segregating into groups unwilling to openly and earnestly talk. But Ethics Bowl gives him hope.

> Democracy dies when citizens have insufficient desire and care to argue with one another respectfully… I take pride in playing a small part in teaching so many young people how to argue together the Ethics Bowl way… Ethics Bowl, as it continues to grow, may help save our democracy.

Ben Sachs, founder of the Ethics Cup in the UK (formerly the John Stuart Mill Cup, named after the famous British philosopher and proponent of Utilitarian ethical theory), shares Matt Stolick's hope and vision, and is inspired to use Ethics Bowl to revitalize and invigorate democratic deliberation.

> To me, it seemed that Ethics Bowl is aimed at inculcating virtues of open-mindedness and the ability to disagree agreeably—virtues that seem to be in short supply in today's democracies... Ultimately, if enough students take part in Ethics Bowl and learn something from it, there will eventually be a critical mass of engaged, open-minded citizens who through the sheer force of the example they set will be able to make salient again the old norm demanding that in a democracy one must listen respectfully to one's opponents and, if one disagrees with them, attack their arguments as opposed to the people who make them.

Ethics Bowl China founder and organizer, Leo Huang, first heard about Ethics Bowl on a philosophy podcast. With a growing interest in philosophy but few opportunities to discuss it with other Chinese high school students, he took the initiative to build that community from scratch.

> I figured that the Ethics Bowl program might be the very chance for such discussions, which later proved absolutely correct: not only did we gather together high school "philosophers" all over the country, our event also became a forum for educators (serving as judges) who either teach philosophy or are interested in philosophical discussions of such. Of course, the Ethics Bowl is by no means a philosophy debate, but its philosophical background is definitely what attracts an organizer like me in the first place.

Leo has since graduated, moved to the U.S. and earned a bachelor's degree in physics from The University of Pennsylvania where he's now a grad student studying neuroscience. Ethics Bowl China is on hiatus as a result. But Leo remains active and is quick to support when asked, recently forwarding translated Ethics Bowl materials to a teacher in China interested in holding local competitions (thanks for your help, Leo!).

You probably have to be a bit of a nerd to get excited about Ethics Bowl. But I'm right there with former Chicago HSEB co-organizer Kelly Laas, who's had the honor of working with Ethics Bowl creator Bob Ladenson, and who shared how she was hooked from her very first Bowl.

> The level of critical thinking, constructive dialogue and collegiality on the part of the students was mind-blowing. The discussions happening before and after

> the competitions were even more exciting, as the conference hallways and elevators were packed with students and volunteer judges carrying on these deep conversations. Students blossomed as tenured philosophy faculty attentively listened to their arguments and critically responded, and I did have to break up a few conversations to send participants flying to their next match as they lost track of time.

People are sometimes hesitant at first. "*Ethics* Bowl?" But Kelly's testimony shows just how much many people enjoy reasoning through tough issues in good faith. And Ethics Bowl is probably so appreciated because opportunities to philosophize this way feel so rare.

Its potential as an outreach tool for academic philosophy and ethics comes up often as a motivator for organizers. Growing up in East Tennessee, I knew next to nothing about philosophy until stumbling into an Intro class in college. And I suspect East Texas, where Greg Bock teaches at UT-Tyler, is just as much of a philosophy desert. Yet Bock has used Ethics Bowl to share the love of wisdom in the Tyler area, and given the event's success, has apparently earned the community's trust.

> Through the years, I've been frustrated with how few people share my passion for ethics, so when I first heard about Ethics Bowl, I had to get involved.

I am the director of UT-Tyler's Center for Ethics now and the Ethics Bowl continues to be one of our major initiatives. It has support from schools across East Texas.

I actually teach as an online adjunct professor for UT-Tyler, and am super proud of how enthusiastically the community has embraced Ethics Bowl, largely thanks to Greg. Given the state's reputation (much like my own state's reputation—deeply red, suspicious of academics, not terribly interested in entertaining views contrary to the dominant narrative, which I've been told is also true of deeply blue states), you might assume Texans outside of Austin (a notorious hippie outpost) would shun an activity that could inspire critical evaluation of cultural assumptions. However, Ethics Bowl is ideology neutral. It favors neither blue nor red. The only people who have anything to fear from Ethics Bowl are those who know in their hearts their views are indefensible.

Still, even when you're justifiably confident, there's always a risk a cherished belief will be exposed as weak or simply unfairly attacked. So doing ethics takes courage, which we'll talk more about in a later chapter. But for now, kudos to all the brave folks who've decided to give it a try. Thank you for your trust. Fellow Ethics Bowlers: remember, as much as we might be personally tempted to push a particular view on pet issues, leave your biases and the usual partisan nonsense at the door. Our goal is clear, honest, cooperative reasoning, not predetermined conclusions. Accept the possibility that we ourselves could be wrong on many things (it's tough, I know!) and be willing to practice what we preach—neutrality, open inquiry, intellectual integrity, and the courage to self-correct.

Someone who knows a great deal about putting progress over ego is longtime leader of Australia's Ethics Olympiad, Matthew Wills. He also knows a thing or two about making ethics extra fun. With dance music intros and an Olympic theme, Matthew brings a showmanship to Ethics Bowl matched by very few. And it's clear to anyone who's had the pleasure of attending a Wills-organized event that he genuinely loves seeing young people enthusiastic about ethics and philosophy.

> At these events there is a palpable level of excitement, confidence, and often excellent skills in civil rational discourse on display. I am no less attracted to the Ethics Olympiad format today than I was thirteen years ago [more than fifteen now] when we took baby steps in holding the first.

I can't say enough about Matthew's commitment, ambition, and perseverance. We're all lucky he fell in love with Ethics Bowl rather than walkabouts or rugby or whatever they do Down Under. Just check out the proud participants at a recent senior (high school-level) Olympiad with teams from Australia, New Zealand, and India, often joined by teams in Singapore, China, Canada, and the U.S.

A RECENT ETHICS OLYMPIAD GROUP PHOTO *COURTESY OF ETHICS OLYMPIAD*

The one organizer who rivals Matthew's knack for Ethics Bowl fun is Jeanine DeLay of A2Ethics and the Michigan HSEB. Their opening ceremony: a parade. Their first-place trophy: the Hemlock Cup. A recent musical innovation: the first Ethics Bowl rap. Yes, the first Ethics Bowl rap.

In her personal life, Jeanine has successfully run a marathon on every continent, including Antarctica. She helps organize Zoom-based ethics discussions in the offseason as well as Ethics Slams, an Ethics Bowl variant for adults often held in bars (yes, bars—more on Ethics Slams later). So, when I asked her to talk about why she gives so much of herself to ethics and Ethics Bowl in particular, leave it to Jeanine to include in her response a friendly challenge to one of our core values.

> While the much-talked about virtue of civility and how to be civil is included as a benefit, I believe that Ethics Bowl is most beneficial when students are allowed to ask why civility is a virtue in the first place; under what circumstances might it be ethical to challenge certain traditions of civility; and how it is that we might create a civil world that includes everyone, and not just the arbiters of civility. Ethics Bowl provides a forum to conduct this careful scrutiny of all values and ethical practices.

She's right. Decorum can indeed be used as a tool of oppression. Imposing a regime of good manners could deflect just demands for change, for sometimes contacting your congressperson and following proper channels just isn't enough. As much as Ethics Bowl practices and preaches peaceful discussion, an unquestioning insistence on civility no matter the urgency or stakes could indeed unintentionally facilitate injustice.

Oregon HSEB organizer and Portland State philosophy professor Alex Sager, whom we'll hear from again in chapters 5 and 8, has published on a related topic in his academic scholarship.

> Disciplinary norms in philosophy encourage us to either eliminate or suppress our emotions… While we must scrutinize our emotions, the fact that anger is not always apt does not mean that it never is. Numbness and exhaustion are more treacherous than anger.

Indeed, while my favorite ideal ethicist—Star Trek's Spock—usually keeps his emotions in check, he isn't a robot. Fed up with schoolyard bullies, there's a scene in the 2009 movie where a young Spock snaps, tackles, and pummels the worst of them. He later carries on a romance with everyone's favorite communications officer, Lieutenant Uhura. And his friendship with Captain Kirk (Jim) is legendary in terms of their mutual trust and allegiance, despite their complicated work relationship.

When it comes to actual ethicists, we most certainly are not unfeeling automatons. In fact, our innate moral sense, which is expressed through our emotions, is an essential input into the moral reasoning process. We all naturally engage our heads and our hearts when making moral decisions. Ethicists just slow down and do it more methodically.

All that said, Alex and Jeanine would not be Ethics Bowl organizers if they didn't care deeply about the peaceful pursuit of justice. Even in cases where action is warranted, I'm certain that both would advocate for responsible escalation, seeking solutions and choosing civil disobedience long before violent revolt. But the fact that they'd challenge us to think hard about the downsides of civility and emotional restraint, while continuing to serve as two of Ethics Bowl's most dedicated and tireless champions, is all the evidence we need to prove that our organizers are an especially thoughtful and cool bunch.

And if we're talking about Jeanine DeLay, we have to mention her faithful protégé, Gabe Kahn. Before he joined A2Ethics as an intern in 2016, Gabe had "never experienced a true ethics lesson (or even philosophy in general)." But Jeanine could see his potential. Thinking back, she sensed his integrity and even temper. And (*tip for our students*) unlike many intern applicants, Gabe "actually listened to the questions we asked him in the interview."

A University of Michigan senior at the time, A2Ethics soon entrusted Gabe to help organize the Michigan HSEB and an Ethics Slam. It didn't take long to confirm he was in the right place. Today, almost a decade later, Gabe's appreciation for the power of applied ethics has only grown.

> Rather than minimizing nuance for the sake of winning an argument, ethics forces us to enhance and build upon each other's arguments so that regardless of who scores more points from the judges, each side ends the conversation understanding the topic better than they did before. In a sense, ethics forces us to consider every complex issue from multiple sides so we both learn more about the issue and ourselves at the same time.

Having long ago graduated out of his intern role, Jeanine is proud to call Gabe "a treasured board member… the director, keeper, and innovative force behind the A2Ethics Virtual D.Y.O. [Design Your Own] Ethics Symposia Series." In addition to his Bowl organizing support, Gabe's led Zoom-based ethical discussion series on AI, abortion, the death penalty, and more. As an attendee and invited speaker, I can personally confirm that anything he puts together is top-notch. Three cheers for Gabe! A rising Ethics Bowl superstar who made an impression by actually listening in his intern interview.

Finally, if you've had the thought, "This organizing thing sounds awesome… I'd be so proud of myself, and it's so consistent with my values, but I'm just not sure I could do it," I want you to remember how Gabe had never even studied philosophy—let alone ethics—before coming aboard. But even more importantly, I want you to remember two words: Max Minshull.

Max approached me in 2014 with interest in launching the Southern California High School Ethics Bowl. I was on the other side of the country in Tennessee, but was used to supporting new organizers long distance as the National High School Ethics Bowl's Director of Outreach. Max and I worked together via phone and email, recruiting teams, judges, moderators, and other volunteers. Max helped convince none other than the University of Southern California to host. And when Bowl day arrived, I flew my family out to serve as his backup organizer, just in case he needed the support.

This is cool, but wouldn't be especially remarkable or inspiring but for one key fact. At the time, Max was a high school junior. To this day, he's the only high schooler I know of to organize an Ethics Bowl. And Max didn't just organize it. He founded the thing.[28]

[28] It didn't hurt that Max has awesome parents. Special thanks to family friends Lee and Sandii Minshull for putting my family up at the Disneyland California Hotel while we were there. My kids still have the stuffies you gifted.

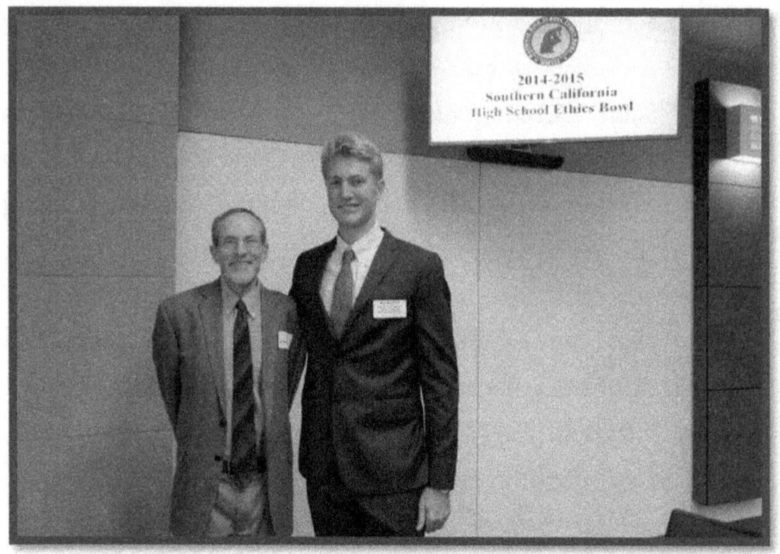


**MAX MINSHULL WITH ETHICS BOWL CREATOR BOB LADENSON AT THE 2014-2015 SOCAL HSEB** *I ACTUALLY TOOK THIS PICTURE :-)*

Since then, Max has graduated from Stanford with a degree in history, fallen in love and gotten married, and today works as a historic car broker, competing on the weekends as an amateur racecar driver in everything from Porsche 911s to desert buggies. He's also 6 foot 6, blonde, and surfs. Obviously, Max is a unique, talented, impressive dude. He and international marathoner Jeanine DeLay should meet! But the fact that Max could found and organize an Ethics Bowl as a high school junior proves it's very much doable. If you have the interest, if you feel like you'd be proud of yourself, and if it's consistent with your values, go for it.

## Case Writers

However, if a behind-the-scenes role sounds more your speed, we're always in need of quality case writers. The next chapter is devoted to Ethics Bowl's cases, and we'll talk about what makes for good ones (hint: no easy answers). But first, meet Michael, Chris, and James.

University of South Florida philosophy professor Michael Funke has been a fixture of the Ethics Bowl community for as long as I can remember. When I reached out to interview him, he reminded me of just how long it's been.

> Matt, I first met you at the original [Association for Practical and Professional Ethics] interest meeting in [a national high school Ethics Bowl]. You and I were both grad students in a room full of full professors. I was impressed with your excitement about the Bowl then and am impressed with your dedication. Thank you for all your efforts. You rock!

I must say that the admiration is mutual, and that Michael has done far more rocking for far longer. On the IEB level, Michael began coaching in 2002, has been a judge at regionals and nationals, began writing cases in 2007, and has continued doing so ever since. He's stuck around for the fun and the benefits for civic discourse. But he was originally drawn to Ethics Bowl by the commitment of a team. While lesser mortals might have fled this group's sunrise symposia, Michael was inspired to join them.

> As a young graduate student, several students approached me about coaching a regional team. This was before the regional system fed into the national Bowl and this group could only meet at 6 a.m. When they explained this to me, I was impressed with them and excited to work with them. This excitement for learning, for discussion, for philosophy, is why I continue to support Ethics Bowl.

I've stayed up late to judge Bowls in other time zones. But consistently meeting in-person at 6 a.m. to coach? That level of dedication is truly extreme. Thank you for all of your efforts, Michael. I'd like to know where those beastmode IEB team members are today. But whatever the case, *you* most definitely rock. Be on the lookout for good ideas from Michael in chapter 9: Ethics Bowl's Future.

Case committee contributor and judge Chris Ng is another longtime devotee, who recently signed on as co-organizer of the Northern California HSEB. But she initially saw Ethics Bowl as a way to share philosophy with younger students, and to empower them with the ability to formulate and spread quality ideas.

> The Ethics Bowl allows young people to explore their beliefs about ethics and how the world should be,

> and it helps them build confidence in expressing those ideas to others and to allow their ideas to be challenged by others.

And like many Ethics Bowl enthusiasts, Chris sees Ethics Bowl as a way to share philosophy more broadly, to make it possible for more students to begin studying it sooner, and for that opportunity to exist independent of a student's economics, geography, race, or any other arbitrary factor.

> The deeper that I dove into my graduate studies in philosophy, [the more] I realized how doing philosophy improved my ability to think critically, not only in my academic studies but also in my everyday decision-making, and I wished I had started studying philosophy at an earlier age… My vision for the future of the Ethics Bowl is for it to be available to all high school students, especially to underserved communities.

And finally, as a member of his IEB team at San Jose State, James Day enjoyed and grew from examining Ethics Bowl cases. Prep required imagining how a reasonable critic might challenge his team's view, which revealed moral blind spots and helped him see issues in a new light. But today as a philosophy graduate student at Purdue University and the IEB case committee chair, James finds writing cases even better at expanding his perspective.

> After writing a case, I usually find myself unable to make a claim about what the appropriate response to some issue or situation might be. My intellectual curiosity and intellectual humility are constantly being developed as I write new cases, and the process expands my worldview and humanizes my (potential) opponents. I wouldn't give up case writing for anything.

Case committee members like James, Michael, and Chris share a special responsibility. A case set's topics must resonate. Each case's details must be clear. And as James emphasized, their presentation must be neutral and any preliminary analysis balanced.

The result of their dedication—and the dedication of dozens of case writers like them—is a rich library on topics ranging from online dating to organ harvesting, student privacy to segregated proms, plantation weddings to Tiger King. However, rest assured that Ethics Bowl is sensitive to age differences. We're much more likely to introduce elementary school kids to Daniel Tiger than Joe Exotic. But any controversy is fair game. The tougher and timelier the better. And it is to Ethics Bowl's cool cases which we now turn.

# CHAPTER 5

# THE CASES!

While teams may begin meeting as early as they like, the Ethics Bowl season doesn't truly begin until case set release day. Traditional debate formats often only provide teams a list of topics and positions such as, "The United States should pay all adult citizens a universal basic income."[29] But Ethics Bowl goes to the trouble of publishing a fresh set of self-contained page-long briefs every regionals and finals season. Thanks to the care of case writing committees, each will include key facts, contrasting mini-arguments, and discussion questions allowing teams to begin their analysis immediately and to concentrate on the ethics rather than outside research.

I'll typically skim the titles to get a feel for the topics, fingers crossed for a mention of Artificial Intelligence or something related to bioethics, then print a hard copy and read them one by one. I'll capture the main thrust in the margins, jotting down which values seem most prominently

[29] For a quick example of how Ethics Bowl frames the idea of a universal basic income, which may become more important as AI increasingly disrupts the economy, visit nhseb.org/case-library/universal-basic-income

in play, which parties stand the most to lose, and which analysis angle might bear the ripest philosophical fruit. Then I'll set aside a favored few to comment on at EthicsBowl.org to kickstart teams' thinking. Not to suggest anything definitive. But simply as a starting point for teams—especially new teams—to consider, critique, and take in new directions.

A favorite high school case, "Sperm of the Dead," asked whether it would be OK to use your zygotes to conceive if you unexpectedly died. If you were hit by a bus tomorrow morning, would it be OK for your spouse to extract your sperm or egg from your dead body and use it to conceive?

Decide for yourself, but I argued that the answer would depend on your express wishes.[30] Control over our zygotes' fates may cease once voluntarily released, especially when voluntarily released in proximity to conception-enabling counterpart zygotes. (New coach tip: high school cases involving reproduction are rare, but when they do come up, using technical terms can blunt the embarrassment of anything related to s-e-x.) But unless you've expressly shared a desire for your kids to be conceived after your death, it wouldn't seem kosher for anyone, even a close loved one, to use them for that purpose.

30 EthicsBowl.org/2017/10/31/2017-2018-NHSEB-case-15-the-sperm-of-the-dead/

Again, this was from a high school case set. There's way Ethics Bowl would broach it with younger students, and the wording was especially professional, despite the cheeky title. But hopefully you agree that this is an interesting moral dilemma—one without an easy answer and worthy of thoughtful discussion.

## What Makes for a Good Ethics Bowl Case?

Quality cases are timely and tough, yet accessible. The issues are relevant, solutions nonobvious. Crafting an engaging storyline takes time. The Sperm of the Dead case was fairly simple, featuring three brief paragraphs on bereaved wife Amy and late husband Bob. But properly conveying their story, which noted unease from Bob's family about Amy's desire to move forward with the "posthumous sperm retrieval" procedure, required both skill and time. And so when a final regional case set goes public in September, it's because case writers have been drafting, cross-editing, tweaking, and finalizing for months. (Today, maybe AI can speed things a little with proper expert oversight—more on ethical ways to leverage AI for Ethics Bowl in chapter 10: CheatBot or SuperTutor?) The result: ten to fifteen tight one-pagers, complete with citations and discussion prompts.

A case's scope can be confined to the interpersonal, sweep across domestic policy, go full international, or tie together all three. Stakeholders might include family, neighbors, countrymen, future generations or animals in faraway lands. The values in tension may not be clearly comparable. How should a team balance honesty vs. happiness, privacy vs. loyalty, autonomy vs. care? As an ethics professor, I'm not always 100% sure myself. As Ethics Bowl coach and Vancouver School of Arts and Academics philosophy club advisor Jon Lauderbaugh explains, that the answers to many ethical questions aren't simple is the point.

> Ethics Bowl's case studies help students to realize ethical quandaries that are challenging and, rarely—if ever—either/or propositions. As such, the case studies challenge students' worldview(s) and help them to develop more refined thinking. Ethics Bowl cases also help students to realize that quality reflection and insight is real work… The consequence is that they understand that there are few obvious answers to Ethics Bowl case studies, and that ethical thinking takes real time and real effort. Furthermore, they find that this hard work, this hard thinking, is well worth their time and effort. In short, they learn and enjoy what Ethics Bowl offers them. The work creates meaning and substance for them.

Teams might have to consider the impact of a decision on the economy, the environment, the international order. Career vs. family, identity vs. empathy, progress vs. contentment. Ripped from the headlines, borrowed from Disney+. While the words used may be refreshingly brief, the ideas behind them run deep.

Case writers strive to come across as neutral as possible. No matter how badly they might want an issue decided a certain way, neither judge, nor coach nor participant should be able to tell. Issue framing is balanced, terms neither euphemistic nor dysphemistic. Readers should never think, "The author of this case was obviously a Rawls worshiper…" or "What twisted nihilist conservative penned this?"

While philosophical concepts are almost always in play, allusions to them are discreet. As I mentioned in chapter 2, Ethics Bowl pioneer Pat Croskery always clarified that "It's not *Theory* Bowl," meaning teams needn't invoke Kantianism to earn high marks. However, whether people are being treated with adequate respect is a legitimate question. The same for whether they're behaving true to our tacit commitment to rational consistency, which Kant formalized with his Categorical Imperative. But countless humans have intuitively applied these concepts having never read a lick of Kant, and while Ethics Bowl case analysis does require clarity and consistency, it requires zero philosophical technicality.

The best cases also affirm that reasonable disagreement is an unavoidable fact. Certain influencers tell us that those who disagree with their tribe are either ignorant, stupid, evil, or all three. But thinking through the best Ethics Bowl cases reveals how equally caring and intelligent people with the same information can arrive at conflicting conclusions. In this way, the Ethics Bowl experience gently tempers arrogance. As Oregon HSEB organizer Alex Sager puts it, sooner or later, participants can't help but realize smart people can disagree with them in good faith.

> The cases are genuinely difficult. When I lead training workshops, I point out that reasonable, informed people disagree about every case. Students learn to analyze and research the cases and come up with a position that takes into account other perspectives. This is not easy to do—among other things, it means becoming comfortable with ambiguity and uncertainty. Too often schooling is structured only to find the right answer, which means either eliminating topics where there isn't a clear right answer or ignoring reasonable disagreement. This doesn't prepare children for life, which can't be reduced to multiple choice examples of fill-in-the-blank responses.

While all Ethics Bowl cases are challenging, the varied authors' styles and backgrounds tend to produce a range of complexity. This makes intentional case pairing on Bowl day important. Good organizers will match cases of comparable difficulty and even theme within the same round: public policy vs. public policy, interpersonal vs. interpersonal, professional ethics vs. professional ethics. That way teams are tested and judged on roughly the same thing. This isn't always possible, but it is preferred.

When I've organized, I've also tried to save the tougher cases and racier topics for the semi-final and final rounds. That way newer, less confident teams can feel comfortable and competent early in the day, and judges should have an easier time identifying which teams are truly best towards the end.

## Kickstart My Heart (and Head)

While philosophical ethics isn't rocket science, it can be intimidating at first. Yet it's manageable (and fun) for those of us who've been studying and teaching it for a while. That's why a big part of the mission of EthicsBowl.org has been to give teams, especially new teams and new coaches, expert support. I've enjoyed offering modest guidance on how to teach ethics, prepare for Ethics Bowl, and think through particular cases there for a decade or so. It's nothing fancy—just a part-time blog. But I like to think it's helped sustain the movement and built a little momentum.

However, I'm just one dude, with a limited perspective and other things to do. And so I was thrilled when high school Ethics Bowl coaching rock star, Michael Andersen, agreed to join the team as a writer. In addition to case analysis and how-to coaching articles, Michael has shared dozens of case study guides, complete with links to related videos, updates from regional and national organizers, and even connections to cases from past seasons. Sometimes he'll even throw in a mini-scrimmage overview so teams know what to expect at practice.

VSAA Philosophy Club
Agenda
~ 1-25-24, 4:05-5:20 pm ~
EB Case #16
Is Watney Worth It?
(HS Only)
(MS see item 2 below)

1. *Welcome, Intros, Brief Club Business* (5 min > 4:10)
   - ☐ Avoid future suffering by organizing your remaining prep time now!
   - ☐ **Vital Logistics Detail:** OEB Letter to Parents **(share and discuss at home)**

2. *Case Analysis: #16 Is Watney Worth It? (HS) ... OR refining any previous case for the MS team (#14, #05, #03, #09, or #02)*

   *Case Analysis Process:* (55 min > 5:05)
   - ☐ **Choose a 2 recorders to make notes on the back of the Guide**
   - ☐ **Aim to complete steps 1-8 today of** the Step-by-Step Guide **for Case 16**
   - ☐ **Begin drafting your** Minimum Presentation Plan **<-- First, make a copy!!!**
   - ☐ **Make a record of questions your team has about:**
     - the case description and Discussion Qs;
     - the stakeholder's views and moral tension between parties;
     - what you need to feel more confident about your team's position statement on the case and your analysis of it.

3. *Wrap Up - Large Group Share*
   - ☐ **Highlight insights so far about Case 16 + review steps 3-8 of** the Step-by-Step Guide **+ share draft position statements** (15 min > 5:20pm)

AN EXAMPLE OF HSEB COACH MICHAEL ANDERSEN'S STUDY GUIDES SHARED AT ETHICSBOWL.ORG *PAGE 1 OF 5*

I've dabbled in coaching. But I've never been especially organized or thorough. Michael, on the other hand, is top-tier. His team in Washington state is super lucky to have him, and thanks to his unusually selfless generosity, coaches and participants around the world are as well. Can you think of another activity where coaches publicly share their game plans weeks beforehand? There's no way I'd tell an opposing soccer coach I'd be running a 3-2-3 formation with a high attacking center back and a goalie good enough to block a shot, dribble out of goal, weave downfield, shoot and score (my son Noah could do exactly that when he was little, winning many games for coach Dad). Michael, on the other hand, puts it out there for everyone to see, including coaches and teams he'll face in the Oregon Bowl at Portland State. I suppose most of his resources don't fully disclose his team's exact position. But they sure offer strong clues, and give opposing coaches everything they need to prepare.

However, such is the spirit of Ethics Bowl—growth and community over winning. Here's some insight into why Michael does it.

> I appreciate how much the regional and national cases each year track and refine the national dialogue on the social, political, and economic issues that divide us. Ethics Bowl helps foster clarity about these issues, the conflicting moral intuitions that drive controversy about them, as well as what it means to participate actively as a citizen. I believe that only

> through a process of wisdom-driven reflection, introspection, and critical analysis together—in learning communities like Ethics Bowl—are we more likely to unify our country and foster better relations with people who live and think differently.

Indeed, that cases do not shy away from hot topics is another mark in their favor. For an idea of their breadth and coolness, here are some examples of articles with the "case analysis" tag at EthicsBowl.org, either with an accompanying article from me or a study guide from Michael.

> **"Factory Farming,"** on the often cruel treatment of chickens and other commercialized animals, which gave me an excuse to feature a picture of Napoleon Dynamite wrangling hens. It also provided an opportunity to plug grad school buddy (and now Loyola University assistant professor and Intercollegiate Ethics Bowl team coach) Joel MacClellan's "Size Matters" argument that all else equal, it's less wrong to eat creatures that produce more meat. Arguing from the perspective of a Utilitarian committed to maximizing net pleasure, Joel might prefer we abstain from meat consumption completely. But if you're going to dine on flesh, beef is better than bunny, whale better than quail.

**"Well, That's Debatable,"** about whether questions concerning topics such as the efficacy and safety of vaccines, the roundness vs. flatness of Earth, and the possibility that certain politicians are actually vampire lizard people should be considered "closed" and unworthy of further public debate. Michael provided a thoroughly comprehensive review of this case on the site, but in my introductory comments I humbly argued that for philosophers, no questions are closed, though some can be moved through more quickly. For example, whether Ethics Bowl is better than debate seems quite settled. But Jeanine DeLay's point about civility sometimes stifling justice deserves additional discussion.

**"Boy, Bye: Or, On the Ethics of Ghosting,"** on the contemporary courting practice of cutting off relationships without explanation. I've been out of the dating game since 2001, so can't really comment. But while I'm sure being ghosted stings, at least one comedian has pointed out that it's better than the old-fashioned method of having your love interest meticulously detail your every flaw to your face.

**"I'm Afraid,"** on the implications of creating sentient artificial life, which I connect back to early human life and abortion ethics arguments, though not too much. Few are truly interested in abortion ethics, though for those who are, I can recommend a decent book...

**"Our Baby, My Body,"** about a couple's disagreement over whether the pregnant woman should risk contracting COVID, possibly endangering their future child's health. While case committees are usually extra diplomatic with wording, I argued this title wasn't as neutral as it should have been—hinting at a possible pro-choice bias—offering in its stead, "Properly Balancing Parental Autonomy During Pregnancy." Not nearly as catchy, but hopefully less divisive.

**"Nandi's Choice,"** about a young immigrant torn between finishing grad school in the U.S. or returning to India when his father dies to care for his mother. Pitting personal ambition against familial obligations, staying would mean higher long-term earning potential. Going would mean honoring familial expectations and cultural norms.

**"Foreign Activists,"** on the ethics of outside influence on domestic elections, which left me torn. Just how committed to democracy are we? For example, if the Taliban's subjection of women were truly the will of the Afghan majority, would that be reason to look the other way? And what about my own government's historical anti-democratic meddling in Central America and Iran? It seems hypocritical to complain about Russian or Chinese interference here without chiding the CIA for doing the same abroad. And maybe we're less serious about honoring the will of the people than doing what's right, at least when the two clearly conflict, which is an interesting topic given the purpose of this book. Just how committed to democracy are we?

**"Is It OK to Punch a Nazi,"** on the temptation to excuse political violence when the victim's values are in stark contrast to your own, an increasingly important topic, inviting increasingly vital reflection.

**"Belief vs. Action,"** on leaders not practicing what they preach—environmentalists traveling via private jet, religious leaders living lavishly, ethics professors glamorizing combat sports – that sort of thing.

In addition to my and Michael's takes, guest articles are always welcome. Please reach out if you or your team are interested in contributing. It doesn't have to be perfect—we'll help edit.

For example, Arsheen Sarani wrote a nice piece on "The Korean Pop Industrial Complex," about the pressures of the young and famous to succumb to grueling schedules, cosmetic surgery and near-perfect performances to please record execs. Luis Villanueva wrote on "Dining Out During a Pandemic," about a decision many of us faced in 2020, with implications for people with compromised immune systems, as well as hospitality industry workers.

NOVEMBER 12, 2018

# 2018-2019 IEB Case 10: Poverty in Paradise

*The following guest analysis is from DePauw University Intercollegiate Ethics Bowl team member, Marko Mavrovic. If you or your team would like to author a guest analysis on either an IEB or NHSEB case, we'd be pleased to share it. Scroll down to review which cases have already been covered, and email matt (at) mattdeaton.com to confirm the submission details. And thanks for leading the guest analysis charge, Marko!*

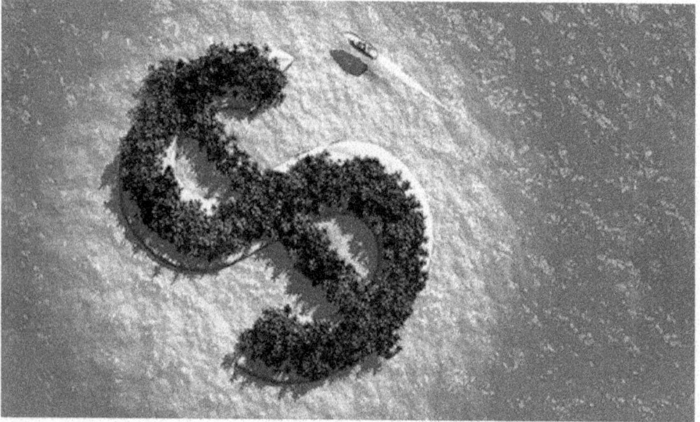

Criminal individuals and corporations utilize the secrecy and fiscal leniency of small island tax haven nations to store their illegally-obtained assets. Some of these assets have been gleaned from developing countries via various means. Given this, the connection between tax haven nations and the further impoverishment of developing countries warrants closer inspection.

**EXAMPLE OF A GUEST CASE ANALYSIS AT ETHICSBOWL.ORG**

*IF YOU WOULD LIKE TO WRITE ONE USING YOUR ORGANIC HUMAN BRAIN, PLEASE REACH OUT.*

We'll also occasionally feature brief video analyses. NHSEB regional case "Plantation Wedding" was about using former plantations as wedding venues. Insensitive and tacky for sure. But some argued that repurposing the beautiful estates for happy occasions could be a way to celebrate progress.

Shortly after that case set went live, a house near my home in Tennessee went on the market that was rumored to have been occupied by Union troops during the Civil War. A friend picked up a sales flyer, and while quartering Yankees wasn't mentioned, that its bricks had been kiln-dried by enslaved people now buried on the premises, was. The macabre selling point was presented neutrally, and how a potential buyer might take it was left to interpretation. Would they envision sipping mint julip and reminiscing old times not forgotten? Or would they research the families who worked the farm and build a memorial?

Now more than six years since that case was released, I drive by that house at least twice a week, and the only change I've noticed from the new owners is a life-sized statue of a buffalo in their front yard, as well as another of Santa Claus on their front porch that stays up year-round. Why a buffalo rather than a reindeer, I'm not sure. I'm scared to stop and ask. But I did mention the house's slave-dropping sales pitch in a brief YouTube video on the case as another example of how past tragedy can be exploited for contemporary profit, context that hopefully enriched a team discussion or two.

## The Case Summary Matrix

You're getting an idea for how diverse and complex Ethics Bowl cases can be. Up to fifteen can be a lot for teams to digest, analyze, and be prepared to discuss. So one recommendation to coaches and teams I've shared is to create a "case summary matrix." Fancy name, but it's really just an organized table.

In the first column, type out each case's number and title. In the second, summarize the basic facts. In the third, the key moral details. In the fourth, an initial analysis. And in the fifth, a preemptive response to a critique of that analysis. If you think back to the way an Ethics Bowl round unfolds, you'll notice how this follows what you'd find on a typical score sheet. Judges are prompted to ask themselves three questions when evaluating a team's initial speech:

a) Was the team's presentation clear and systematic?
b) Did they appreciate and clearly articulate the case's central moral dimensions?
c) Did the team's presentation indicate both awareness and thoughtful consideration of different viewpoints, including those that would loom large in the reasoning of individuals?

Fifteen cases is still a lot. But a concise case summary matrix gives teams something to help track progress during the weeks leading up to a Bowl, plus something to cram the night before and reference between rounds. While I was never the best coach, I do think using a case summary matrix helped my teams. So if you decide to lead one yourself, give it a try.

## Pressure to Pick Perfect Cases

When I hear about a promising but potentially dangerous development in biotech (such as advancements in artificial wombs) or a friend passes a novel new law (high school buddy turned Tennessee state house representative, Lowell Russell, sponsored a bill that revokes teenage bullies' driving privileges), I think, "This would make for a great Ethics Bowl case! I shall now email and irritate my case committee contacts."

But when I do this, I realize committees can't accept all idea pitches. They're only human, and in addition to having limited time and energy, they have to be mindful of the message including an issue sends. Even when presented evenly and objectively, simply including a topic suggests it presents a live moral question worthy of thoughtful discussion. Ethics Bowl cases are supposed to be reasonably interpretable from a variety of angles. So if the right thing to do is truly obvious to almost everyone, that means it should have been judiciously omitted.

I didn't think too much about this until an IEB coach friend who prefers to remain anonymous brought it up. She explained how a phenomenon called the "Overton Window" (no connection to brilliant historian cousin and beta reader, J. Overton) refers to the scope of acceptable public discourse in any given society. Radiating outward from the status quo, ideas range from *popular* to *sensible* to *acceptable* to *radical* to the completely *unthinkable.*

Since Ethics Bowl cases are expected to be difficult to resolve—meaning the central moral tensions could be reasonably decided differently—my friend argued that including a topic in a case set suggests the solution must be nonobvious. Further, the case set itself could be interpreted to imply that Ethics Bowl leadership believes these are *the* hot issues ethically-minded people should be discussing this season.

> The case packet signals to participants both that each case is individually worthy of their consideration, and that this set of cases are the issues worthy of consideration that year, or at least sufficiently and representatively worthy of consideration that year.

She mentioned one case in particular that seemed to re-open an issue she believed had been closed shut years ago.

> The 2023 case packet's opening case, "They Yearn for the Mines," asked students to (re)consider child labor, an issue the American public litigated a century ago, thanks to Arkansas Governor Sara Huckabee's desire to put the profits of meat packing

megacorporations operating in the state she governs over the wellbeing and education of Latino children cleaning slaughterhouses on school nights. Suffice it to say that teams did not exactly rush to defend child labor.

In addition to suggesting child labor might be OK—a claim my friend contends is glaringly false—the case wound up enabling groupthink. During prep, her IEB team quickly concluded child labor should not be allowed. And she suggested teams at IEB regional competitions did as well, leading to less than fruitful discussion that round.

In the IEB case committee's defense, there apparently have been a significant number of legislators pushing to expand employment for younger workers. The case's footnoted sources include the USA Today article, "Lawmakers in 11 States Seek to Weaken Child Labor Restrictions" and another from the Associated Press, "Kids Could Fill Labor Shortages, Even in Bars, If These Lawmakers Succeed." 11 states, including Ohio, Minnesota, and Tennessee, is significant.

A lawmaker in Tennessee (not my buddy Lowell) said changes were needed to address staffing issues in the hospitality industry in particular. So it's a relevant issue that on the Overton Window scale apparently isn't *unthinkable* or even *radical* in some policymakers' minds. And since it's being openly proposed, they must consider it at the very least *acceptable,* if not *sensible* or yet widely *popular.*

However, in defense of my friend's critique, IEB competitors, coaches and judges probably are indeed inclined to prioritize childhood education, safety, and innocence over work experience and income. I'm sure there are exceptions. But a unified rejection of kids working in slaughterhouses or Roadhouse-style dive bars seems predictable given their self-selection to participate in the IEB.

Whatever you think of the issue, I'm simply happy to share the Overton Window and point out how difficult and important our case committees' work truly is. Case committee members: thank you! We know it ain't easy. I did a little work with the NHSEB case committee, so know firsthand. Your behind-the-scenes dedication isn't unnoticed, and the community appreciates the care you take to deliver engaging and balanced cases season after season, elevating many of our most important contemporary issues and inviting some of the most thoughtful minds in the world to tackle them. My anonymous IEB coach friend may not appreciate you (kidding!). But the rest of us most certainly do.

## Check 'Em Out

Current and past case sets are openly available online. APPE hosts an IEB case library with regional and national sets from the 2001 season through present at appe-ethics.org/cases-rules and NHSEB hosts regional and national sets from the inaugural 2013 season through present at nhseb.org/case-library. Both are searchable by topic, which makes using Ethics Bowl cases in your classroom especially easy. I regularly include them in my in-person college classes, both Ethics and Intro to Philosophy (more frequently in ethics classes than others), and students love how they make what can be an abstract subject immediately practical.

If you're an educator, pick a favorite and give it a try. For younger students, search for Middle School Ethics Bowl cases or Ethics Olympiad junior school cases. Usually at a page each and with built-in discussion questions, ten minutes from now you can understand the allure. Because while Ethics Bowl's format may be our core advantage over traditional debate, it's the thoughtfully crafted cases that keep enthusiasts hooked. And apart from engaging students who might otherwise be tuned out, Ethics Bowl just might improve their standardized test scores.

# CHAPTER 6

# IT IMPROVES TEST SCORES?!

While you might agree that rejuvenating democratic norms is an urgent need, most of us are understandably more concerned with our day-to-day responsibilities. The chief baker at Dunkin' Donuts may dream of expanding "hole" foods into "underglazed" communities (ha!). But when it's time to make the donuts, making donuts takes precedence.

When it comes to school administrators deciding whether to encourage, allow, or veto the formation of a new Ethics Bowl team—or to support transition to Ethics Bowl from tried-and-true traditional debate—similar pressures apply. Attendance, pass/fail rates, and government-mandated test scores often override most everything else.

So if Ethics Bowl is to successfully grow and transform our culture, we'll need to be able to tout benefits that resonate with those in charge. And one benefit sure to catch their attention is the possibility that Ethics Bowl improves standardized test scores. The case isn't ironclad. But the link is plausible enough and definitely worth sharing. And this is especially true thanks to a late-breaking study by two researchers named Michael in North Carolina.

## It Improves Standardized Test Scores?!

Whether there's a direct link between Ethics Bowl and better grades is arguable. But at least one study suggests philosophical discussion does have an impact. Here's an excerpt from a handout I developed while serving as the National High School Ethics Bowl's Director of Outreach targeting principals while recruiting new high school teams.[31]

> While instructors have suspected for years that doing philosophy sharpens cognition in a way likely to impact standardized test scores, it wasn't until 2007 that researchers confirmed this hunch with a series of studies conducted in Scotland.
>
> Drs. Keith Topping and Steven Trickey found that 10-to-12-year-old students who participated in one hour of weekly philosophical discussion improved their verbal, non-verbal and quantitative scores on the widely respected Cognitive Abilities Test (CAT3, 2001) by an average of 7 points, compared to a control group whose scores remained steady.

[31] Enduring thanks to Roberta Israeloff of the Squire Family Foundation for sponsoring my fellowship, and to our partners at the University of North Carolina's Parr Center for Ethics for getting the NHSEB off the ground including Jan Boxill, Geoff Sayre-McCord, and Katelin Kaiser. Look at our baby now!

Especially exciting was the finding that ***gains made during the initial 16-month study continued in the experimental group two years after the sessions had stopped,*** while the scores of the control group marginally declined.[32]

Further, analysis of video recordings and student questionnaires administered seven months into the study revealed increased participation, better behavior, and self-reports of greater confidence, empathy, and control.[33]

Whether similar results could be achieved by Ethics Bowls is yet to be determined. But Topping and Trickey's findings give us good reason to think pre-college philosophy supports the interests of a test-centric academic culture.

Admittedly, that study wasn't specifically about Ethics Bowl. But Ethics Bowl certainly requires philosophical discussion, and many of those who know Ethics Bowl best are convinced it benefits students as students. For example, Glendora High School Ethics Bowl coach Pat Hart in

32 "Collaborative Philosophical Inquiry for School Children: Cognitive Gains at 2-Year Follow-Up," British Journal of Educational Psychology (2007), 77, 787-796.

33 "Collaborative Philosophical Enquiry for School Children: Participant Evaluation at 11 years," Thinking: The Journal of Philosophy for Children (2007), 18(3), 23-34.

California has concluded from years of coaching that it helps students improve both their Advanced Placement class grades and their college entrance exam scores.

> Preparing and delivering an Ethics Bowl presentation via the three judging criteria aligns seamlessly with the College Board (AP classes and SAT) rubrics for both long and document-based essays. Furthermore, the emphasis on critical analysis found on all of the exams goes hand-in-in with the skills practiced in preparing cases for an Ethics Bowl. This is not simply my observation—my students point this out to me each year. So… without data to support, (but I am 100% correct) Ethics Bowl helps students perform better on their AP exams as well as the SAT.

Coach Pat recruits and works with some of Glendora High's best and brightest. He writes letters of recommendation for his students applying to colleges every year, and went on to share something I didn't expect but was thrilled to hear—that Ethics Bowl experience is beginning to be not only recognized, but prized, by entrance committees.

> I have noticed recently that university admissions who have reached back out to me to further discuss a candidate DEFINITELY now know what Ethics Bowl is—and this has proved vital to helping prove

to a university that they are considering a very strong critical and analytical thinker who can speak and have tough conversations with their peers. What other experiences in your average high school provide this benefit at this level?

## Hold the Presses!

If you're encouraged by Topping and Trickey's work and coach Pat's testimony, but discouraged that this is the best we can do, would a multi-year analysis covering *over half a million* undergrads from *800 U.S. colleges and universities* help? Thanks to the extended labors of Michael Prinzing of Wake Forest and Michael Vazquez of UNC, your wish is my command.

Published by the Journal of the American Philosophical Association in 2025, *barely* in time to be included in this book, the Michaels sought to scrutinize the claim that studying philosophy boosts test scores. Using mathematical wizardry and a fancy stats program called "R," they isolated test performance improvement by comparing college majors' average law school (LSAT) and grad school (GRE) entrance exam scores relative to students' pre-college SAT scores. That way, they'd reveal not whether students who gravitate to philosophy happen to be good at taking tests (they apparently are), but whether studying philosophy improves test-taking ability. In other words, they sought out to answer whether phil majors became comparatively better at standardized test-taking over the course of college, compared to students of comparable pre-college ability who studied other subjects. For good measure, they threw in student self-reports on scholarly virtues to see which college majors attracted and cultivated the most serious students. How did philosophy fare?

> Our results indicated that students with better verbal reasoning abilities and more curiosity, intellectual rigor, and open-mindedness are more likely to major in philosophy. They also indicated that, after adjusting for baseline differences, philosophy majors outperform other students on these measures. In fact, on average, philosophy majors score higher than all other majors on the GRE Verbal and LSAT, as well as a self-report measure designed to assess good habits of mind.[34]

If you take a look at the study, which is openly available online (just google the title: "Studying Philosophy Does Make People Better Thinkers"), flip to page 11 to see philosophy majors at the tippy top of the adjusted average LSAT scores table—ahead of political science, history, chemistry, and all flavors of engineering. On the GRE Verbal table, philosophy beats every major again, including languages and literature, and even English. On the GRE

[34] "Studying Philosophy Does Make People Better Thinkers," Journal of the American Philosophical Association, published by Cambridge University Press, 2025, page 13.

Quantitative, philosophy is middle of the pack, but certainly not at the bottom, and primarily behind math-heavy majors including mathematics/statistics, physics, computer science, and accounting, though somehow business administration and management beat us (dang it…).

The study is brand new, and maybe some future criticism will reveal flaws. Plus, I'm predisposed to want it to be true, and you might be as well. But it sure seems credible, even if the methodology is way over my head (mixed-effects regressions for dichotomous outcomes with random intercepts—*what?*).[35]

Independent of whether we're fluent in Statistician, thanks to Vazquez and Prinzing, when we pitch Ethics Bowl and philosophy to administrators, we now have a recent, broad, ultra-impressive study to cite. And the news gets even better. I reached out to the Michaels for their help with this section, and they shared that Ethics Bowl-specific test score improvement studies are on their research agenda. Shoot yeah. Thank you, Michaels!

35 "Our analyses used mixed-effects regression models (logistic regressions for dichotomous outcomes) with random intercepts for institutions (i.e., the colleges and universities that students attended). We fit these models using the *lme4* and *lmerTest* packages in R (Bates et al. 2020; Kuznetsova, Brockhoff, and Christensen R. H. B. 2017), computed estimated marginal means using the *emmeans* package (Lenth et al. 2018), and used multiple imputation to accommodate missing data with the *mice* package (Buuren and Groothuis-Oudshoorn 2011). The code used in these analyses is available online (https://osf.io/4S693)," ibid, page 7.

## Shout it from the Rooftops?

I think most any potential advantage that will make Ethics Bowl more appealing is worth sharing. Make a plausible case that it builds lean muscle mass or kills mosquitos or finds lost car keys, and those are perks I'm going to tell others. However, on the better grades thing, some will worry that appeasing the test trackers is antithetical to Ethics Bowl's purpose.

For example, Ethics Cup organizer Ben Sachs in the UK does a nice job explaining how the Ethics Bowl format is treasured for its ability to encourage open-mindedness and autonomous learning, and how it's explicitly *not* about getting better grades.

> Ethics Bowl inculcates an extremely important civic virtue: toleration of those who disagree with you. It also encourages students to study philosophy and ethics, and gives them an opportunity to engage in self-driven learning, which is to be contrasted with instrumentalized learning, where the ultimate object is getting a good grade.

Helping students cultivate empathy for others and an inner love of learning is more than enough to inspire me, and is probably more than enough to inspire you. But for better or worse, data-driven metrics rule the day, and non-STEM subjects are increasingly undervalued. One reason is that we live in an age when tech dominates both markets and battlefields. And when companies and governments are paranoid they'll be overtaken by rivals, time spent on non-STEM material can feel like time recklessly squandered.

Plus, there's a related anti-expert, anti-intellectual, anti-humanities undercurrent that's been growing for some time. Harvard political philosopher Michael Sandel writes eloquently in his 2020 book, *The Tyranny of Merit,* about how college has served as a sorting mechanism separating the haves from the have nots. Whether intended or accidental, heaping praise on graduates and excluding non-graduates from many positions of power has understandably driven resentment towards anything that smacks of academics or "elites."

He's certainly not the only one to exploit this sentiment, but former U.S. senator from Florida, Marco Rubio, channeled it at a debate while he was running for president back in 2015. And he stuck it to philosophers in particular.

> Welders make more money than philosophers. We need more welders and less philosophers.

Ouch! Welders are definitely important. So are builders, plumbers, electricians, and HVAC professionals. However, there's no reason students who pursue a vocational track can't also dabble in philosophy. But did Rubio have to compare incomes?

Not that it matters (and not that philosophers are sensitive about their pay…), but fact-checkers couldn't help but investigate, and found that the average income of "newly graduated philosophy majors" was within $140 of that of "welders, cutters, solderers and brazers."[36] That's within $140 *annually*. To be fair, soldering and brazering don't sound as fancy as welding, and so including those occupations probably pulled down the group's average. But they only made $140 more than recent phil grads over the course of an entire year? Again, not that it matters…

One thing that does matter is that few will argue with a straight face that most philosophy students should plan to do it for a living. Rather, philosophy teachers will openly, directly, and repeatedly tell their students, "This is *not* a practical major. Double major in something that will pay your bills. Please!" At least that's what my professors told me. So I double majored in philosophy and political science, which left open the possibility of going to law school. Though according to the Michaels' study, I would have done just fine on the LSAT studying philosophy alone.

Obviously, I and many others believe studying philosophy is valuable regardless of occupation. And not just while you're of school age. But it's a false dilemma to suggest you're either a welder or a philosopher. In fact, you can be both.

[36] "Philosophers (and Welders) React to Marco Rubio's Debate Comments," Alan Rapport, The New York Times, November 11, 2015.

## Philosophy for All

After Rubio's original comments in 2015, journalist Alan Rapport found and interviewed a University of Chicago philosophy Ph.D. who, after having trouble securing fulltime work teaching, joined a think tank, then gave that up to become a welder. Well, he became a mechanic with the ability to fabricate and weld motorcycle parts. But close enough.

Matthew B. Crawford actually wrote a bestseller about shifting careers from academia to motorcycle repair—*Shop Class as Soulcraft: An Inquiry into the Value of Work*—and argued that there's far more overlap between working with your mind and working with your hands than many assume. Per Rapport's article:

> [Crawford's book] is devoted to debunking the notion that manual trades are mindless. "The division between knowledge work and manual work is kind of dubious, because there is so much thinking that goes on in skilled trades," [Dr.] Crawford said.
>
> As for the payoff, [Dr.] Crawford rejects the idea that philosophers cannot figure out how to earn a living. "It's obviously kind of a reductive approach to think of your course of study in college as merely a means to a paycheck," [Dr.] Crawford said, suggesting the study of things like happiness can be enriching in ways that are hard to measure. "And nobody goes

> into philosophy because they think it's going to make them rich."[37]

We'll revisit the question of whether studying philosophy can have positive benefits for your finances next chapter. But notice how much respect Crawford conveys for blue collar work. I'm sure education snobs exist. But from my experience, academics respect plumbers, welders, etc. far more than the politicians who attempt to pit us against one another suggest. I've worked in factories. I've sealcoated parking lots. I haven't forgotten. The divisive myth that college grads are foreign to and have nothing but disdain for non-grads is probably part of the reason vocational training and STEM subjects are being prioritized at other subjects' expense. And this unfortunate trend isn't unique to the U.S., as explained by Ethics Olympiad judge Dirk Baltzy.

> As I write this, the Australian federal government is considering a change to university fees that would see tuition for subjects in Philosophy and History increase by 113%, while tuition fees in Science, Technology, Engineering, and Mathematics go down. The future, our politicians believe, is all STEM, all the time.

37 "Philosophers (and Welders) React to Marco Rubio's Debate Comments," Alan Rapport, The New York Times, November 11, 2015. I'm not sure why, but the article repeatedly calls Dr. Crawford "Mr.", which I corrected. Not that philosophy Ph.D.s are sensitive about that... or their pay...

However, while many government officials may underappreciate the value of non-STEM studies, Baltzy goes on to share the good news that our brothers and sisters with the slide rulers actually have our backs.

> If, however, you talk to scientists, they will tell you that technological development needs a strong moral compass. They will tell you that you need to consider the *humans* who will be the users of any technology. You will need to understand them, not merely as the subjects of the social sciences do, but from the inside, as participants in the collective human experience.

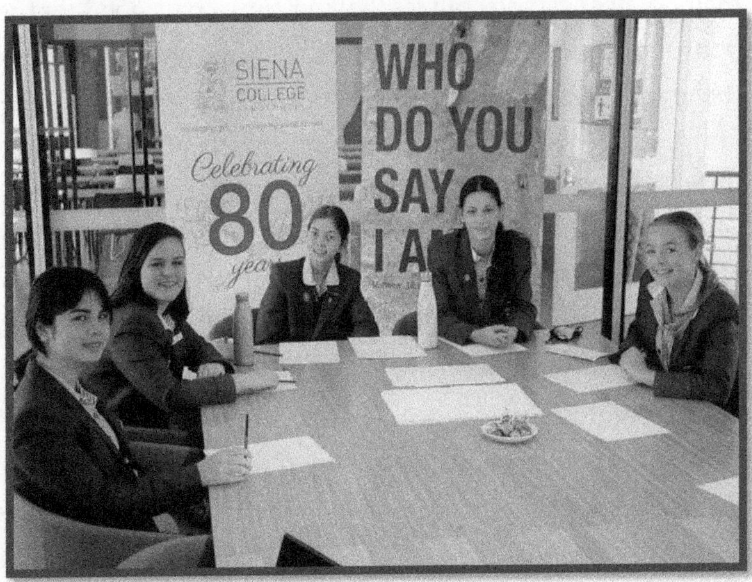


THE SIENA COLLEGE (HIGH SCHOOL) ETHICS OLYMPIAD TEAM FROM VICTORIA, AUSTRALIA, WHO I'M PRETTY SURE DOES WELL ON STANDARDIZED TESTS ALREADY COURTESY OF ETHICS OLYMPIAD

As thoughtful scientists will admit, advancements in empirical knowledge aren't especially useful without accompanying value judgments to tell us how we should and shouldn't use them. But good luck convincing an unsympathetic school administrator under pressure from STEM-biased policymakers. That is, good luck convincing them without evidence that Ethics Bowl may improve standardized test scores.

But even without test score boost evidence, people understand that there's more to life than what's right in front of them. English philosopher Bertrand Russell wrote about the archetype "practical man" who "recognizes only material needs, who realizes that men must have food for the body, but is oblivious of the necessity of providing food for the mind" in his essay, "The Value of Philosophy" in 1912.[38] However, Russell didn't think a too-practical mindset was inescapable. It's clear that we're all more or less philosophical, more or less practical, depending on our changing life circumstances.

For example, Marco Rubio himself was inspired to reconsider his position after reading the work of ancient Roman philosopher Seneca. While he may have wanted fewer philosophers and more welders in 2015, in 2018—after experiencing philosophy firsthand—he humbly updated his evolving view.

38 Available in the final chapter of his *The Problems of Philosophy*.

> I made fun of philosophy three years ago, but then I was challenged to study it, so I started reading the stoics. I've changed my view on philosophy. But not on welders. We need both! Vocational training for workers & philosophers to make sense of the world.[39]

Now *that's* what I'm talkin' 'bout! A skeptic brave enough to try philosophy, admitting they were wrong, and becoming an outspoken cheerleader. Never mind that it took three years. We're all works in progress, and Rubio's conversion is a lovely confirmation that even those who seem most anti-humanities can be brought around.

Super cool that direct exposure to philosophy is what did the trick. Though if you're thinking of gifting humanities critics primary texts, learn from Rubio's excitement and make it Seneca, Marcus Aurelius, or some other accessible, practical text. I'd avoid Kant's *Critique of Pure Reason* (brilliant, but very hard to follow) or anything by Hegel (does anyone *really* understand Hegel?).

## Remember: Improved Test Scores

Whether higher test scores impress you personally is irrelevant, because they do impress decisionmakers in charge of appointing Ethics Bowl coaches and commissioning Ethics Bowl teams. And thanks to Topping and Trickey, and especially thanks to Michael Vazquez and

39 From @marcorubio on Twitter/X, March 28, 2018.

Michael Prinzing, we can play that game.

Keep their work in mind as you broach Ethics Bowl with administrators, colleagues, potential volunteers, participants, and parents, as well as coach Pat Hart's confidence that Ethics Bowl is helping our participants prep for college entrance exams and impress admissions boards. For all young people deserve to know what philosophy is, they deserve to be invited to discuss philosophical and ethical questions, and they deserve to be guided by dedicated educators in an environment of calm inquiry.

Ethics Bowl achieves all of this and more, possibly boosting GPAs as a happy byproduct of Shaping Tomorrow's Ethical Minds. How's that for our own STEM catchphrase! I have to credit collaboration with AI on that one. I could have gotten close, but **S**haping **T**omorrow's **E**thical **M**inds is just too clever for this organic human brain to think up solo.

More on responsible use of AI in chapter 10: CheatBot or SuperTutor? But first, a few thoughts on Ethics Bowl as a way to improve our participants' career and financial decisions—another possible side benefit increasing its chances of rapid adoption. Now, how to prove that Ethics Bowl kills mosquitoes…

# CHAPTER 7

# CAREER AND CONSUMPTION WITH A CONSCIENCE

There's a tendency among those of us with a soft spot for philosophy and ethics to shun careerism, consumerism, materialism, and the like. Similar to how education should be valued for its own sake, moneymaking should be a tolerated necessity, not life's primary aim. This seems wise and enlightened, and I tend to agree. However, pushing a life of the mind that's too detached from practical realities risks alienating our participants.

For example, Diogenes, an ancient Greek so proud of his ascetic lifestyle that he lived disheveled in a barrel, was an interesting character. He once threw away one of his few possessions, a cup, when he saw a boy drinking water with his hands, complaining, "a child has beaten me in plainness of living."

There aren't many philosophy or ethics teachers glamorizing *this* level of extreme minimalism. But there's a definite anti-money bias in the humanities, which we have to work through to best connect with our participants. The reason is that our culture will condition them to chase cash on some level whether we like it or not. And so we do neither them, the humanities, nor the public at large any favors by struggling in vain (remember the "Noble Loser" from chapter 1?) to convince them money is inherently dirty or that the only ethical paycheck is a small one.

To be clear, I'm not suggesting we run in the other direction, into the arms of The Simpsons' Mr. Burns or the Wolf of Wall Street. But I am suggesting we should be open to and appreciative of Ethics Bowl's ability to help participants make better life choices, including life choices about how they earn and spend.

## Advanced Degrees, Advanced Careers

IEB-winning coach Mike Ingram of Whitworth University in Spokane, Washington was introduced to Ethics Bowl by colleague Keith Wyma in 2003. As Ingram reflected on the disposition and skills Ethics Bowl would foster, he quickly realized its real-world value. Not only would it improve participants as students, but as professionals.

> The preparation and research skills that students could develop would help them with classes now and careers in the future. The need to organize ideas and create a systematic presentation was important and would promote clear thinking. Working with a team of peers would foster good interpersonal communication skills and prepare them for the workplace of the future.

Now with years of Ethics Bowl experience and documented success as a coach, Ingram even better appreciates how it enhances participants' higher-order reasoning, teaching them comfort working with nuance and ambiguity, which are traits valuable in most any context. And similar to how high school coach Pat Hart reported Ethics Bowl helping his students prepare for and get into college in chapter 6, Ingram reports the same in terms of Ethics Bowl preparing his undergrad college students for graduate school—consistent with the Michaels' findings—and the higher-paying careers grad school enables.

> They examine cases with actors who are clearly acting in unethical ways, and actors who may be both morally praiseworthy and condemned at the same time. This fosters the development of greater scrutiny, and sometimes holding conflicting ideas in tension... Several Bowl alumni report the writing portions of the Graduate Record Exam and similar graduate school admissions tests are often quite similar to composing an Ethics Bowl case analysis. This helps open the door to admissions and scholarships. Students gain experience in critical thinking, application of theories to real world problems, and learn teamwork in the Bowl that helps them immediately and in future studies and careers.

This is Ingram's well-informed impression as a champion-level coach. But for a participant's perspective, DePauw University IEB national champion captain Marko Mavrovic was told by friends that Ethics Bowl would help him prepare for law school. And it did. But he didn't anticipate just how powerfully it would improve his reasoning and elevate his ambition.

> Repetition of mantra does not suffice. One's own strongly-held opinions are put to the test. Suppressed premises and commonly-held assumptions are scrutinized. Arguments are critically evaluated. It is a challenging intellectual sport. But the required mode of critical thinking has greatly sharpened my own skills in argumentation and analysis. Indeed, I apply the inquisitive and curious mentality of an Ethics Bowler to my own research and, in doing so, I have set (and met) a higher standard for the work that I produce. As I have told my coach several times, nothing has had a greater impact on me as a student and a thinker than Ethics Bowl.

Now that's a quote worth repeating: "Nothing has had greater impact on me as a student and a thinker than Ethics Bowl." Equally impressive is how Ethics Bowl has inspired Mavrovic to set and meet a higher standard for his work—presumably including non-philosophy and possibly non-academic work—a benefit with far-reaching personal and professional implications.

While I'm primarily excited about Ethics Bowl's ability to revitalize civic friendship, develop citizens' critical thinking skills, model cooperative inquiry, and generally lead to a more just, stable, democratic world, there's no reason it can't benefit participants in other ways as well. If it makes them better students, great. If it makes them more successful professionals, cool. And if it so happens they become more conscientious shoppers, too, even better. For doing so would seem fully consistent with the philosophical tradition.

## Ownership vs. Possession

Rumor has it that ancient Athens featured an open market, no doubt filled with merchants hawking shiny trinkets. It's said that Socrates loved to visit and peruse the aisles, not because he was a shopaholic, but because it reminded him of all the things he was perfectly happy to live without.

Now, that was Socrates. I've been doing this philosophy thing for a long time and still buy far more crap than I should. But purchases consistent with our values are better than impulse sprees, and philosophy does help us better understand, evaluate, and refine our values. In fact, here's a cool argument I often assign my Phil Intro students.

Philosopher John Hardwig is more famous for his end-of-life ethics work, but also published an article on becoming a wiser shopper. He argued that the mindset of modern consumerist society, that more and newer is always better, is not only the enemy of the environment, but just plain stupid.[40] It's stupid because simply having things, even admired things, does little to enrich our lives. Acquiring the latest envious gadget may feel cool at first. But that coolness quickly fades.

Hardwig argued that the reason is that while laying legal claim to an object may enable bragging rights, mere passive ownership is ultimately dissatisfying. Yet, you're still stuck with the bill. On the other hand, buying stuff you'll actively use—especially stuff you'll actively use to develop your talents and enrich your life—produces far less remorse.

For example, lusting after a new Ferrari-style Corvette is understandable. I'm guilty. But at three times the cost of a roomier and more reliable Honda Civic, only donate your finite resources to the Chevrolet dealer if you truly intend to (safely) push a Corvette's technical limits and improve your driving skill. That said, for Ethics Bowl organizing teenage prodigy turned racecar driver Max Minshull from chapter 4, the Vette could be an authentic purchase, though I understand he's partial to Porsches. For me, an F-150 makes more sense given how RV camping is a big part of my family's culture. Myrtle Beach is a favorite

[40] ""Ownership, Possession, and Consumption: On The Limits of Rational Consumption," Journal of Social Philosophy, Vol. 46 No. 3, Fall 2015, Wiley Periodicals.

Independence Day camping spot, but we've also driven "Ebony" all the way to Death Valley, California, Key West, Florida, and Quebec City, Canada. I've even navigated downtown Manhattan (no camper that trip), rollercoaster ridiculous curvy overpasses near Dallas (yikes), and a whirlwind that looked like a mini-tornado in remote New Mexico. Ain't no Honda Civic pulling our camper through mini-tornadoes in New Mexico, though I sure would prefer a Civic's fuel efficiency.

Another illustration for my fellow public speakers and conference presenters: only buy a fancy wireless headset microphone if you'll use it frequently at venues with compatible sound systems. I learned the hard way that while TED talkers make headset mics look super cool, hand-helds get the job done, are far less prone to glitches, and are almost always provided for free by the host. I would love to use my Shure high fidelity wireless mic more often to enhance my presenting prowess. But I usually can't, and so that wound up being an unwise purchase.

Something I should have remembered before clicking Buy Now: an old book by non-philosophers that made a lasting impression, *Your Money or Your Life* by Vicki Robin and Joe Dominguez. It boils down to the simple idea that the more you spend, the more you have to work to pay for it. If you can discipline yourself to buy less, you can work less and have more time to do the things you enjoy.

This dovetails with Hardwig's argument, for one implication of fewer and wiser purchases is that rather than working overtime to pay down your Prime Day splurge, you can spend that time mastering the guitar on a flame-kissed Stratocaster, perfecting your yoga poses on a Manduka PRO instructor-grade mat or sharpening your top pocket soccer finishes on an Open Goaaal bungee net with built-in rebounder (coach Dad recommended). Hardwig isn't pushing a hardcore minimalism that's tone deaf to the pressures we all face in consumerist societies. He's not denying that sometimes it's OK to buy the best when an item truly aligns with who you are and can take your passion to the next level. But he is recommending we align our purchases with our enlightened interests.

Of course, this is coming from a guy who's covering a mortgage, two car payments, an RV payment, a gym membership, way too many streaming services, and untold kids' extracurricular fees by working a fulltime job and teaching philosophy as an adjunct for two different colleges. Books generate a little bonus income, and occasional speaking gigs do as well. But you'll have to trust that I routinely reevaluate my work/spend habits, and that they've withstood some degree of ongoing Socratic scrutiny. (Update: Thanks to Mr. Musk's federal workforce chainsaw of random savings, I'm now teaching philosophy and writing fulltime. Time to carefully reevaluate those spending habits! And/or speak more, write more books…)

Exposing students directly to Hardwig's argument or another like it would help them get the idea faster. But my bet is that Ethics Bowlers become more intentional about their working life and wiser consumers naturally. Every time an Ethics Bowl team clarifies the values in tension in a case, and every time they balance the interests of the parties impacted, they're developing skills that can help them better balance working, spending, and leisure, and make more conscientious life decisions generally.

Our participants will still work. They'll still spend. But they can do both smarter with our help, perhaps transcending the work-and-spend hamster wheel a little better than we have ourselves.

## Does Philosophy Pay?

Many would consider selling the love of wisdom as a path to riches fraudulent. Most philosophers concede that there's much truth in the old saying, "Philosophy bakes no bread." But at least one businessperson, Washington D.C.-based real estate developer Gary Squire, has a different view.

> Studying philosophy taught me to think clearly and critically about myself and others and to systematically evaluate ideas. Although I did not anticipate this at the time, I use my education in philosophical logic and ethics every day in my business.

Recognizing the profound impact his philosophy teachers had on his life, Gary created the Squire Family Foundation in 2007. For the past nearly twenty years, the Foundation has helped to bring philosophy into elementary and secondary schools nationwide so that more students can take advantage of its many benefits, both personally and professionally. The Foundation is also a proud co-founder of the National High School Ethics Bowl (NHSEB) and PLATO (Philosophy Learning and Teaching Organization).

The host of CNN's "Global Public Square," Fareed Zakaria, lends support to Squire's conviction that training in philosophy can have material benefits. In his 2015 bestseller, *In Defense of a Liberal Education,* Zakaria argues that much of the U.S.'s wealth can be traced to our traditionally well-rounded education system. In addition to attracting global talent, some of whom wind up settling and working here, it's given our graduates a broad understanding of the human experience. Exposure to and critical engagement with a range of big ideas fosters creativity and innovation, enhances communication skill, facilitates acculturation, and builds adaptability—all valuable for a rich human life, but also useful for entrepreneurs, executives, and anyone competing in a market economy.

Many enlightened business leaders agree and believe that it's a shortsighted mistake to discredit and defund the humanities. Zakaria quotes former Lockheed Martin CEO Norman Augustine who argues that what corporate America wants, and what the public at large needs, are technically skilled graduates who have also cultivated emotional intelligence and practical wisdom.[41]

[41] Published by W. W. Norton & Company, page 89.

> [We need] more employees who excel in science and engineering… But that is only the beginning… [W]ho wants a technology-driven economy if those who drive it are not grounded in such fields as ethics?... Certainly when it comes to life's major decisions, would it not be well for the leaders and employees of our government and our nation's firms to have knowledge of the thoughts of the world's great philosophers and the provocative dilemmas found in the works of great authors and playwrights? I believe the answer is a resounding "yes."

ONE PROFESSION REQUIRING SOUND JUDGMENT IS MILITARY LEADERSHIP, SO IT'S REASSURING THAT SEVERAL U.S. MILITARY ACADEMIES PARTICIPATE IN IEB, INCLUDING THIS 2025 QUATERFINALIST SQUAD FROM WEST POINT *COURTESY OF APPE IEB®*

Indeed, when business leaders like Augustine are making hiring decisions, demonstrated success studying philosophy—given the breadth of study and logical rigor philosophy demands—indicates that there's a good chance that a candidate is both more well-rounded than an applicant only focusing on technical skill, and also very unlikely to be unsmart.

In *The Undercover Economist,* Tim Hartford shares how Nobel Prize-winning economist Michael Spence used this example to illustrate a solution to "the problem of asymmetrical information." Fancy name, but really they're just inferring that phil majors are unlikely to be dense.

> Spence... shows that smart, diligent people can prove they're smart and diligent by going to the trouble of getting a philosophy degree... employers are willing to [hire them] despite the fact that the philosophy degree itself does not improve the candidate's productivity at all. It is merely a credible signal, because a philosophy degree is too much trouble for lazy, dumb people to acquire. Since Spence himself majored in philosophy at Princeton, perhaps there is something to his idea.[42]

[42] Published by Random House Trade Paperbacks, 2007 edition, page 111.

You can draw your own conclusions about the likely traits of philosophy graduates. But any support the business community would like to lend Ethics Bowl, we shall not turn away.

However, as a rule, this isn't a typical selling point. Studying philosophy and ethics are intrinsically valuable, apart from any possible material gains. Accordingly, few of us do or promote Ethics Bowl with future affluence in mind. But the clarity and reflection it demands can lead to deeper self-knowledge, peace, personal and professional success. It can help students decide which career options are truly consistent with their considered convictions. It can also help them realize that what "success" means depends largely on their personal definitions, which they'll be in a better position to thoughtfully articulate having participated in Ethics Bowl.

## The Fine Print

One risk of studying ethics too long is that it can make you feel guilty about more than you probably deserve. Maybe we should disclose that as a known side effect… But one known side benefit is that it can improve your life choices, including choices involving money.

If our alumni use the skills we develop to more wisely earn and spend, that's something to be proud of. So we probably shouldn't push back too hard against Squire, Zakaria, Spence, or anyone else who's convinced the humanities, philosophy, and ethics can help our participants professionally ascend and financially flourish.

Just because most ethics educators don't prioritize material riches doesn't mean the love of wisdom can't help people build and live good lives in every sense of the word. For Aristotle himself argued that while we need virtue, friends, and health, we also need a certain degree of material comfort. And as serial entrepreneur and philanthropist Alex Hormozi says in *$100M Offers: How to Make Offers So Good People Feel Stupid Saying No:*

> Anyone who says money can't buy happiness hasn't given enough away.[43]

Yes, we just considered advice from millionaire podcaster Alex Hormozi and the great Aristotle in the same mental breath. And yes, I've read Hormozi's *$100 Million Offers.* While I can't say I necessarily endorse every word, I do applaud Hormozi's philanthropy, and I do recommend his strategy of overdelivering. And as I hope you're coming to agree, Ethics Bowl consistently overdelivers.

[43] Published by Acquisition.com, LLC, 2021, page 69. Hormozi doesn't claim to have originated this clever quote. But free tip for entrepreneurs: he does argue that it's smarter to increase your product's value than reduce its price.

# CHAPTER 8

# BETTER CLASSROOMS, SCHOOLS, COMMUNITIES

Teaching ethics is fun, but isn't always easy. Take Utilitarianism. As straightforward as maximizing net pleasure might sound, every semester a certain number of students will confuse it with hedonism. "Whoa, I should do whatever makes me happiest? Awesome!" "Um, no—it's whatever would bring about the most pleasure overall, which might require sacrificing some of your happiness for the sake of others'." Some mix it up with democracy. "Dude, if the majority wants it, it's moral? Vote for me!" "Not quite—people vote for things contrary to net happiness all the time, sometimes because they're selfish, but sometimes because while they want what's best for everyone, they're mistaken about what that is."

When teaching a concept like Utilitarianism, rather than dealing in abstractions, analyzing a concrete issue helps. It allows an instructor to clarify how all impacted parties need to be taken into account, how intense pleasure (or preference satisfaction) for a few can override mild pleasure for many, and how short-term joy can be outweighed by longer-term misery.

But even then, good luck making progress on anything as complicated as real issues in the real world. Even if you manage to pin down a specific aspect, most topics are muddled by contested facts. "I heard global warming would boost food production. Plus, didn't Joe Rogan prove the earth is flat?"

That's why Ethics Bowl is so helpful for educators. The neatly packaged cases provide enough detail to draw conclusions, but not so much that students get lost. The sample discussion questions offer clues for productive analysis. And the scoring rubric provides ample incentive to think ahead, actively question assumptions and recheck initial figuring. This is of course not only helpful for ethics and philosophy instructors, but any teacher covering contemporary issues or simply looking to boost students' critical thinking in an engaging, practical way.

IEB and HSEB organizer George Sherman in St. Petersburg, Florida appreciates all of these benefits for sure. But even more, he loves how Ethics Bowl helps students combine rational and emotional thinking in ways typical classroom instruction can't. The way George puts it, Ethics Bowl is uniquely maturing, enabling a special kind of authenticity.

> A more vernacular way to describe the effect of the Ethics Bowl is to install a "BS" detector in the minds of the students. In the future, they can detect BS—even their own.

I agree. But leave it to George to frame student growth in terms of boosting their BS detectors!

IEB national championship-winning coach Marcia McKelligan of DePauw University also uses Ethics Bowl to teach, and considers it a special opportunity to challenge promising students. She might go easy in a lower-level undergrad course including non-philosophy majors. But she shared how she uses Ethics Bowl to push students serious about philosophical ethics to the next level. However, it's the ability to open minds McKelligan ultimately finds most valuable.

> Ethics Bowl is still a place where students must acknowledge "both sides" of an issue, which in my judgment, makes it stand out from some other pedagogical environments. Many a student coming to a case with a fixed opinion has changed her mind after working through the case and trying to construct a presentation with solid arguments. That can be a transformative experience for a young person.

Ethics professors may be biased. But the growth we witness year after year—growth that many of us underwent in our own ethics classes (which likely didn't come until college)—feeds students' natural inquisitiveness. As explained by Oregon HSEB organizer Alex Sager:

> It is unfortunate that most schools in the United States don't include philosophy as part of the curriculum, because young people are asking philosophical and ethical questions, but are often not given the tools to begin to answer them. Ethics Bowl opens up a space to reflect and talk about important personal, social, and political topics.

And like other organizers, coaches, and judges, Sager is continually inspired by Ethics Bowl's ability to model highbrow deliberation.

> The level of discourse in the average Ethics Bowl discussion is head and shoulders above the average political debate. I'm heartened by the thought that students participating in Ethics Bowl will take what they learn into their lives as students, family members, and citizens.

This confidence that Ethics Bowl's benefits extend well beyond the teams involved is widely shared. Ethics Olympiad's Matthew Wills of Australia explains how when a school signs up to participate, an implicit raising of expectations follows.

> There are also important extrinsic benefits such as the benefit of schools being seen to take the inculcation of ethical thinking seriously in the school's program. This is also important in that schools signing up for

> the Ethics Olympiad place themselves in a position that they must prepare their teachers and students to engage at a sophisticated level in ethical thinking.

In many places, including where I live, Ethics Bowl is the primary (if not the sole) vehicle introducing the love of wisdom to the public outside of academia. But as participants' and volunteers' attitudes and habits change, they rub off on classmates, family members, and ultimately their communities. This has been organizer Greg Bock's impression with UT Tyler's Ethics Bowl in East Texas.

> Not only are high school kids learning ethics and responsibility, but the volunteers may be encountering ethical ideas for the first time in their lives.

To make the diffusion of Ethics Bowl's benefits even more certain, Mary Helen Wade of the South Carolina High School Ethics Bowl has made a point to invite select community leaders to judge. This not only boosts the prestige of the event for participants, but shows leaders how the rising generation would prefer they behave.

> Here in South Carolina, we believe including judges from the community is important. Yes, we have professors, but at least half our judges are drawn from leaders in the community. One judge said to me, "After judging today for this Ethics Bowl, I have

> renewed faith in our young people!" We feel including members of the community models leadership for the high schoolers, but also allows the community to glimpse how these kids think and how the students reason and explore these challenging topics.

This two-way, students being inspired by existing leaders and community members being inspired by participants, is part of the beauty. And unlike other areas of philosophy, ethics is both approachable and relevant. Ethics Bowl demystifies what can seem an arcane discipline. It shows philosophy isn't necessarily hostile towards religious faith (more on this point towards the end of next chapter). And it opens the door to a world of reflection and growth so many are unaware even exists.

## Good for Philosophy Departments, Too

From the perspective of college administrators and department heads, Ethics Bowl can also help pay the bills. Students like me will continue to stumble into phil courses to satisfy degree requirements. A few will fall in love, switch majors, and stick around until they're given a Ph.D. But as University of Tennessee philosophy professor emeritus and former department chair John Hardwig argues (the same "ownership versus possession" Hardwig from last chapter), hosting a high school Ethics Bowl is also cost-effective way to boost undergrad enrollment.

> Sponsoring an Ethics Bowl has brought our department significant benefits at no significant cost. As an outreach event, it generated visibility and support for philosophy within the community, reaching high school teachers and administrators as well as parents of high school students. It provided our graduate students with an important service-learning opportunity. And it helped to generate interest in our classes among incoming undergrads, since many Ethics Bowl participants eventually enrolled.

Not only can Ethics Bowl enhance a department's reputation and recruit new students by exposing them to the joys of philosophical inquiry, it can empower graduate students to share their knowledge while developing a sense of civic responsibility. As these young professionals spread across the country and work their way into faculty positions, they inevitably reinforce philosophy's connection to the everyday. And whether they realize it, volunteering can enhance their employability. As Ethics Olympiad judge Dirk Baltzy puts it:

> If you're a head of department or chair of graduate studies, Ethics Olympiad is a really good opportunity for your Ph.D. students and recent graduates to both give back to the community and to put something on their CV [resume] under "service".

Fellow Ethics Olympiad judge and Sydney Middle Years Olympiad organizer Andrew Constantino adds how a high school competition can encourage even earlier pre-college study, as well as cross-discipline collaboration. Younger students, along with their siblings and families, far from being excluded, are welcomed.

> Ethics Olympiad has led to interest in the broader parent community and student body. It has enhanced the profile of philosophy at the college. On the back of our success in the competition and the profile it built we are now going to offer an integrated philosophy, psychology and politics course for years 9-10 (13–15-year-olds)… We also teach Philosophy as part of the International Baccalaureate (2 years) and we are integrating Philosophy 4 Children (P4C) pedagogy into a new years 5-6 (9-11-year-olds) program. So much of this became possible because of the interest that this competition initially created. The recent International Olympiad has solidified and renewed this interest.

It should be no surprise that Ethics Bowl also facilitates collaboration with like-minded groups. As explained by Jeanine DeLay, A2Ethics (A2 = Ann Arbor) in Michigan considers their co-founding and co-support of the Michigan HSEB with the University of Michigan's philosophy department a marvelous joint venture.

> Our partnership is a strong and successful example of campus-community collaboration. The A2Ethics volunteers from our community are honored and inspired to be involved with the graduate students, teachers, judges, and students in, what has become for some youth and adults, a transformational program.

Canadian High School Ethics Bowl co-organizer Nick Tanchuk confirms that Ethics Bowl can add to thriving intellectual networks or serve as a catalyst spawning new ones.

> I think that it fosters some of the best things philosophical inquiry has to offer: a way to build community through intellectual engagement, a commitment to flexible and open-minded thinking, and a sense of fallibility in moral matters. As a philosopher who works on educational questions, Ethics Bowl seemed like a positive way to support public philosophical engagement and deepen work that is already happening in K-12 spaces.

More than a stand-alone event, Ethics Bowl can be a gateway further democratizing the discipline and encouraging its inclusion in everyday life. It's a testament to the power of philosophy as a tool for building community, nurturing critical thought, and fostering curiosity. It's equipping participants with skills and understanding to navigate the ethical complexities of the real world. And it's putting undergrad butts in philosophy class seats, creating new jobs for future professors, and fighting the misguided notion that only the hard sciences are worth students' time and tuition.

Later we'll consider an argument from IEB and HSEB organizer George Sherman (aka St. George) that Ethics Bowl should be at the top of any educational institution's extra curriculars list. Sports can build resilience and teach life lessons. Chess can sharpen wit. But we'd be hard pressed to find an activity better at cultivating quality citizens.

Yet, it's not perfect. No one pretends it's perfect, though you might have reasonably inferred that I do. But the good news is that it's not static, either. Ethics Bowl is an ongoing experiment, and leaders regularly meet to consider opportunities for improvement and implement changes when they seem all-things-considered best. So in the next chapter we'll explore a range of ideas for making Ethics Bowl even better, including bolstering guidance on how to handle contested facts, adding opportunities for more direct team-to-team interaction, and the benefits and drawbacks of Bowling online versus in person.

# CHAPTER 9

# ETHICS BOWL'S FUTURE

When I asked Ethics Bowl enthusiasts what they would like to see in our future, some emphasized improving accessibility. Some were all about expansion and growth, both at home and overseas. Others offered ideas for format improvements. One worried about the implications of dancing around contested facts, and another shared deep concern that differences between Ethics Bowl and traditional debate are diminishing. I suspect some of these ideas will gain more traction than others. But one point of near-converging agreement was that almost everyone who mentioned online Bowling was a fan. *Almost* everyone.

## Online = Accessible, Inexpensive, Global

Before COVID-19, Matthew Wills was traveling across Australia to host Ethics Olympiad trainings in thirteen capital cities. In case you've not looked at a globe lately, Australia is huge. Matthew didn't have to trudge through the outback like Crocodile Dundee. But that much travel across that sort of landscape takes a toll.

Bearing that burden firsthand, I suppose it's not surprising that Matthew's been a pioneer of online Bowling. He helped orchestrate a friendly among high school teams in Australia, California, and Tennessee way back in 2010. I know because I was at Austin East High School in Knoxville that night. One early lesson: have a speakerphone on standby in case webcams decide not to cooperate. But Matthew knows better than most online Bowling's potential and benefits, and was fully prepared to switch operations 100% virtual in 2020 to prevent disease spread and accommodate lockdown rules.

> One positive that has come from this is that it opens the event to more regional and remote schools as they can participate via a computer. In preparation for the online format (and in lieu of the cancelled Senior Ethics Olympiads due to COVID) we ran professional development (training) for coaches and judges... followed by online Olympiads for schools around Australasia and later we ran an international online Ethics Olympiad involving students in Australia, Canada, and China.

The National High School Ethics Bowl in the U.S. also had some practice Bowling online before COVID. As the number of states with regional Bowls expanded, NHSEB needed a way to winnow down the qualifiers to make the final event at UNC manageable, which was a good problem to have.

Rather than asking families to travel hours to compete against champions from neighboring states, event coordinator Katelin Kaiser was able to accommodate via webcam, which at the time was an impressive technological victory. It doesn't seem like a big deal today. But back then, Ethics Bowl leaders weren't known for their tech savvy, and it took a young innovator like Katelin to move us forward.

Back then, growth pushed high school Bowls to go partially online. Today, with more collegiate regional champs than can be reasonably accommodated at finals at the Association for Practical and Professional Ethics' annual meeting, the Intercollegiate Ethics Bowl may be facing a similar good-to-have problem. One solution entertained by coach Marcia McKelligan is another qualifying round.

> As it gets more popular, perhaps it will become cumbersome to manage the high numbers. I have thought about a two-tiered qualification structure, but it doesn't seem feasible given how much of the academic year would be occupied if some teams were going to three competitions.

Indeed, an additional layer of IEB prelims could become a pain, further conflicting with participants' and coaches' usual responsibilities. And were it on site, this would negate one of the advantages that drew coach Richard Lesicko to Ethics Bowl from debate. Recall from chapter 3 how he found Ethics Bowl's limited travel schedule a guard against wealthier teams racking up experience most could never afford, as well as a welcome convenience. But perhaps a third tier IEB qualifying round would provide more benefits than drawbacks if held online.[44]

Mary Helen Wade, co-founder of the South Carolina HSEB, does a nice job articulating how remote Bowling also promotes inclusivity and parity.

> I believe that being required to be virtual will be an equalizer, allowing more high schools to participate. We offered scholarships for coming to our Bowl, but even then, transportation was an issue, some students didn't have the clothes to wear to the event and were intimidated to be on a college campus.

Remote competitions not only open doors for underprivileged participants, but allow volunteers to support from anywhere in the world. Bowlers in New York, Shanghai, and Tennessee may have some difficulty understanding one another. But I've found that Chinese students' grasp of English is a million times better than my grasp of Mandarin, and that Northerners and Southerners can communicate just fine with a little patience and practice.

However, while New York and Knoxville may both be on Eastern Standard Time, Austin, Texas and Aukland, New Zealand are not. This is why 8 a.m. and 8 p.m. are popular choices for international Bowls. At 12 hours apart between Pittsburgh and Perth, you're either enjoying your

44 Some IEB programs do travel to different regionals. But Richard found this less common in Ethics Bowl than traditional debate.

morning coffee or nibbling an evening snack. The Americans and Canadians get up early, the Australians, Chinese, and New Zealanders stay up late, and everyone gets to decide for themselves whether the benefits of international friendship are worth the lost sleep (they are!).

Every time I've had the privilege of serving as a long-distance guest judge, the chance to discuss cool cases and network with ethics-minded people hundreds and even thousands of miles away has been a special honor, reaffirming the fact that all cultures are flush with compassionate, peaceful humans. While divisive leaders do their best to scare us with stories of hostile foreigners, international Ethics Bowling, made simple and inexpensive by Zoom, affirms that kindness, reasonableness and philosophical inquisitiveness are universal.

Online Bowling also means fewer event cancellations for snow up North, storms on the coasts, tornadoes out West and down South, and frozen plumbing floods in the Midwest. Yes, frozen plumbing floods in the Midwest. As recalled by Jeanine DeLay of the Michigan HSEB, sometimes water damage can come from within.

> The Bowl venue flooded after some pipes burst about 16 hours before the 2019 Bowl was scheduled to begin. We scrambled and were able to find an alternative venue. And though we were not necessarily "calm," we "carried on." The "2019 Burst Pipes Bowl" is now legend and commemorated in a drawing.

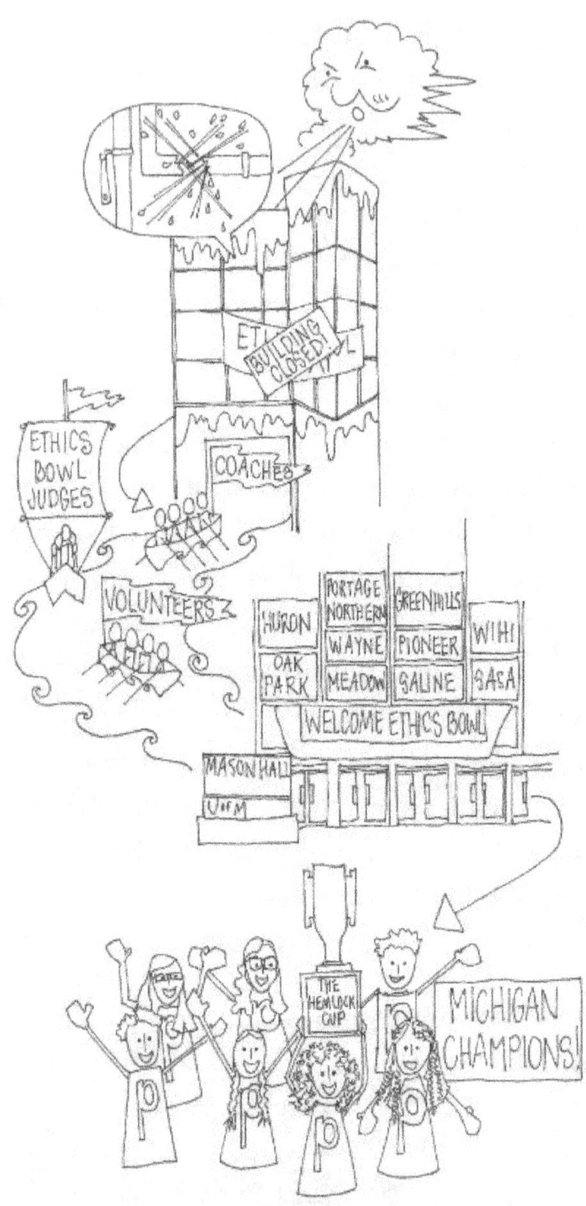


**THE MICHIGAN HSEB "2019 BURST PIPES BOWL"**

*BY ARTIST DUSTY UPTON, COURTESY OF A2ETHICS*

While less resilient organizers would have canceled, of course the gritty Michiganders pivoted and commissioned a cartoon. Artist Dusty Upton does a marvelous job for A2Ethics, by the way, crafting dozens of ethics-themed visuals annually that add extra pizazz to their brand. But the ability to avoid bad weather altogether is a huge perk of online Bowling, and I'm happy to report that options continue to expand.

Both during and since the pandemic, the Parr Center for Ethics at UNC has offered an impressive array of online prep resources for teams. In 2022, their NHSEBAcademy Studio began Zoom-based supplementary coaching. Beyond staffed scrimmages, teams also have the option to book a case brainstorm session, presentation consultation, or practice judge Q&A.

That these sessions are free and available to any team is encouraging. And the case brainstorms are especially promising. It's easy to get sucked into a competitive mindset. Ethics Bowl could use more opportunities for teams to simply share ideas and explore lines of reasoning, and friendly online brainstorms could be one of the best ways to promote the true spirit of Ethics Bowl yet.

Online Bowling can also simply serve as a backup. University of Loyola Chicago ethics professor and Ethics Bowl coach Jennifer Parks shared at an Ethics Bowl workshop how the college Bioethics Bowl, an annual event focused on issues in medicine and health science, pivoted to Zoom to dodge COVID in 2021. Scheduled to be hosted at

Oklahoma State, rather than risk canceling and lose expansion momentum, it made sense to temporarily move the event online, then reconvene in person the following season.

Ethics Bowl Canada's collegiate Bowl holds its eight regional qualifiers virtually, the winners of which travel to a rotating host university for an in-person national championship. And while most of IEB's events are in-person, DePauw University's Prindle Institute for Ethics hosts an online regional for up to eighteen teams.

> First established in 2021, IEB Online is designed to provide a premiere Ethics Bowl experience for students and teams who prefer an online experience, or who are unable to travel for participation in more traditional APPE IEB Regional Competitions.[45]

IEB is also especially good about offering online prep resources—videos on what Ethics Bowl is, how to organize, judge, prepare and participate, sample Ethics Bowl class syllabi (yep, for-credit college classes devoted specifically to Ethics Bowl), live Zoom-based summer workshops for existing and aspiring participants, coaches and organizers on both the collegiate and high school levels. Sponsored by the Association for Practical and Professional Ethics, visit APPE-ethics.org/resources or simply search on YouTube to

45 prindleinstitute.org/community/ieb-online

check out the "ABCs of the Ethics Bowl" videos starring longtime Ethics Bowl royalty, former IEB chair Richard Greene and IEB chair-elect Rachel Robison-Greene. There's even a link to a Google Docs Scrimmage Interest Sheet for coaches to connect and practice online.

From Matthew Wills coordinating an international Ethics Olympiad friendly in 2010 to IEB summer workshops today, the old geographic limitations have been thankfully overcome. However, there are Ethics Bowlers who still strongly prefer participating in person.

For example, Glendora High School coach Pat Hart—who testified in chapter 6 that Ethics Bowl helps his participants prepare for and get into college—shared how his team all but demanded that they participate in the Southern California HSEB on site. The virtual thing was fine during COVID. But once the pandemic subsided, they were eager to shake hands and look people in the eye once again.

> The kids were adamant that they wanted to see other teams face-to-face and in-person. I remember what one of my kids mentioned: "This isn't gaming—it's more like a sporting event—it needs to be completely personal for the real experience." I'm sure I am in the minority on this point, but I am voicing a strong sentiment that was unanimous and made very clear to me by my student Bowlers.

That coach Pat's students so strongly wanted to be in the same physical room as their discussion partners, judges, and moderators, suggests they truly love it, about which we cannot complain. Plus, most of us pay better attention when we're together (harder to "multitask") and the intimacy of in-the-flesh presence just can't be replicated through a screen. I wouldn't say Ethics Bowl is like a sporting event. But it's certainly more like a sporting event than an online video game, and the sincerity expected is indeed more likely to materialize when everyone is breathing the same air.

There's definitely still a place for face-to-face Bowling, and probably always will be. However, the inclusivity, affordability, convenience, and long-distance connectivity of online Bowling are all huge advantages in its favor. Fortunately, there's room for the community to continue to do both.

## Firm Up the Facts

In his book, *On Tyranny: Twenty Lessons from the Twentieth Century,* historian Timothy Snyder warns of the danger of tolerating factual relativism. In an age where BS professed with gusto regularly attempts to upstage inconvenient realities, Snyder argues we're enabling an environment of vanishing accountability when we don't insist that our leaders, press, and fellow citizens commit to shared standards of evidence.

> Believe in truth. To abandon facts is to abandon freedom. If nothing is true, then no one can criticize power, because there is no basis on which to do so… You submit to tyranny when you renounce the difference between what you want to hear and what is actually the case… Post-truth is pre-fascism.[46]

When it comes to fact-checking, there are some differences between Ethics Bowl and traditional debate. While traditional debate expects teams to conduct outside research, Ethics Bowl cases are typically designed to be self-contained, which creates tacit agreement that teams should grapple with the details on the page and focus on the moral elements. This doesn't eliminate quibbling. But it does decrease it. And when a key detail is contested, thought experiments are welcome. Politicians may refuse to engage in hypotheticals. But good Ethics Bowl teams know there's nothing wrong with a well-framed provisional conclusion.

However, Fort Lewis College philosophy professor and author of *Beyond Fake News: Finding the Truth in a World of Misinformation,* Justin McBrayer, argues that Ethics Bowl could do better in this regard, and that our failure to more clearly guide teams on how to navigate empirical disagreements undermines our participants' progress.[47] For

[46] 2021 Graphic Edition, illustrated by Nora Krug, chapter 10.

[47] Much of this exchange was published at EthicsBowl.org on

even among people with shared values, it's tough to advance on an issue without shared facts.

> Even if two people share all and only the same ethical values, they might come to radically different decisions about how to behave and what is right and wrong. That's because they might be starting from different viewpoints about what is true or how the world is. So just as we need Ethics Bowl to help people think through their value commitments, we need a focus on applied epistemology so that people can think clearly about what the world is like.

Ethics Bowl cases at least implicitly attempt to minimize factual disputes by offering enough details for teams to draw conclusions. Just as it's not Theory Bowl, it's not Research Bowl, and no one wants it to become Research Bowl. However, McBrayer argues that if we're to keep the discussion focused on ethics, and if we want to encourage truth-oriented expectations, teams need clearer guidance.

> If we stipulate certain non-value facts at the outset, that will focus the attention on the values in play. But from my limited experience, Ethics Bowl cases don't do a good job of this. They need to explicitly say

August 12, 2022 in "How Factual Assumptions Drive Moral Disagreement and What Ethics Bowlers Can Do about It – an Interview with Justin McBrayer."

> things like (a) assume that 10,000 people will be harmed by this product each year or (b) the company's decision will produce X amount of greenhouse gas or (c) the consumer is aware of the fact that the product is nutritionally useless. If we make it really obvious that teams can't challenge those opening assumptions, the dialectic will be directed towards the value propositions that animate various applied ethical dilemmas.

I agree with McBrayer that Ethics Bowl cases are often empirically ambiguous. And when teams' factual assumptions diverge, so too can their moral conclusions, which can stifle what could have been a productive discussion. Plus, given how fidelity to factual reality is becoming increasingly important in our political environment, Ethics Bowl teams could use additional encouragement to deal in reality. But I suspect one reason case writers haven't been more heavy-handed on the facts is that depending on the issue, doing so could alienate and prevent some teams from participating at all.

On issues where reality itself has been politicized, taking a stand in the case details could cause participants, coaches, and entire institutions to dop out. Were event organizers to preemptively discredit an entire tribe's worldview, anyone sympathetic to it would understandably feel disrespected, assume Ethics Bowl was rigged against them, and decline to participate. But those are people we want and *need* to engage. Ethics Bowl is about big-tent collaboration across ideologies and groups. We can't scare away potential friends by demanding they leave their sincerely-held beliefs at the door. At the same time, we can't invite and tolerate obvious BS. So, what's the solution?

If our cases aren't going to take hard stances on contested facts, and if they're going to continue to leave space for teams to challenge the facts our cases do include, McBrayer offers advice on how to listen for, appreciate the impact of, and be able to effectively navigate empirical disagreements.

> Insofar as a case does NOT stipulate a certain non-value fact, we should encourage teams and judges (a) to recognize the non-value assumptions each side makes, (b) offer challenges to those assumptions and (c) offer objections that ask the other side how their conclusion would change if the non-value facts were altered in such-and-such a way. While we don't want to go too far down the road of having teams try to evaluate and determine non-value facts (e.g. is pollution the main driver of climate change?), we DO want them to see that applied ethical conclusions typically rely on a non-value premise in the argument. Change that premise, and you'll change what follows from your moral principle.

Factual challenges of course already happen at Ethics Bowls, and how a team responds can quickly reveal just how committed they are to the Ethics Bowl way. A judge will say, "You seem to be assuming X causes Y. But what if it were conclusively proven that X does not cause Y? How would that impact your position?" Great teams will have already considered this twist and can respond quickly. Strong teams will confer and make a good faith effort to adjust their conclusions. And weak teams will double down, refusing to entertain the possibility that the facts could be otherwise. It all ties back to humility and a willingness to reason collaboratively.

So I join McBrayer in encouraging our coaches, teams and judges to listen carefully for differing factual assumptions and to press for clarity. If nothing else, go ahead and stipulate facts and work from there.

> Abortion, climate change, vaccines, or just about any other polarized issue works. If you assume the vaccine is effective, then such-and-such follows. If you assume it's not, then… Again, a difference of belief about non-values often lies behind what seems like intractable moral debate. And I agree with you that we don't want to make it a research bowl. But we can do a better job of being cognizant about how our non-value assumptions often drive our value conclusions.

A team's willingness to loosen their grip on a favored claim—especially a favored claim that's been sincerely called into question—says a lot about their commitment to Ethics Bowl's cooperative model, which we of course believe will lead to more cooperation in the public sphere. For agreeing to assume something for the sake of argument, while simple, does signal that you respect and are taking your interlocutor seriously.

To better encourage this, perhaps something could be added to judges' scoring rubrics along the lines of, "The team's factual assumptions were clear and they noted how their moral conclusions might vary were key facts proven different." Or, "When presented with hypothetical changes to key facts, the team was willing and able to adjust their moral reasoning."

And while we want to reinforce the expectation that we all rationally pursue the objective truth, we probably shouldn't ask our judges to score teams based on their assessment of teams' factual assumptions, at least when they're in the ballpark of things a sane person might believe. There may be times we have to be extra generous in deciding what might pass as a sane belief, lest we allow our own certainty to poison an otherwise friendly and conciliatory event. Send the message, "Facts matter, and truth isn't relative." But don't pretend Ethics Bowl is Truth Bowl or overzealously punish a team that happens to profess a worldview contrary to your own.

## Across The Country and Around the Globe

Welcoming and fairly judging teams with differing worldviews is likely to become more important as Ethics Bowl continues to expand, often in ways few could have predicted. For example, as explained by co-organizer Estelle Lamoureux, the Canadian Ethics Bowl accommodates both English and French-speakers, and is branching into Indigenous communities.

> We are currently expanding the Ethics Bowl across Canada in both official languages. We have established a consortium with university organizers... We have also had a preliminary meeting with Australia, Scotland, the U.S., and China on a possible international collaboration. We are also starting to discuss creating an Indigenous Ethics Bowl. The demand is there.

Sensitive to cultural differences and committed to honoring them, Lamoureux envisions an Indigenous Ethics Bowl that speaks specifically to that community's issues and honors their norms. And she's in good company among organizers interested in building a global network. Despite what our more xenophobic leaders suggest, there are of course reasonable, peaceful people in every country. And surprise, surprise—many of them gravitate to Ethics Bowl.

One standout leader in the global Ethics Bowl community is Ethics Olympiad founder Matthew Wills. While we had coordinated via email and webcam since 2010, receiving the prestigious Winston Churchill Fellowship in 2013 allowed Matthew to travel to the U.S. to see the inaugural National High School Ethics Bowl at UNC in person. When we finally shook hands that weekend, I could tell he was a big thinker. But I had no idea he would design and implement such ambitious expansion.

Thanks to Matthew, Ethics Olympiads, which are essentially the same as Ethics Bowls, quickly spread across Australia, initially on-site, but eventually moving all online. And as Matthew and his team perfected Bowling via the online format, this not only allowed teams to join from across Australia, but other countries. He's welcomed newcomers not only in Australia, but New Zealand, China, England, India—not to mention the U.S.

And now, after coordinating with Ethics Bowl stakeholders in the U.S., Ethics Bowl Canada, and Ethics Cup in the UK, he's running international competitions with regionals in different countries serving as qualifiers. International Ethics Bowls were something almost everyone wanted, but only Matthew had the follow-through to do. One reason might be his cosmopolitan sensibilities. He's proven consistently culturally astute, impressing Ethics Bowl China founder Leo Huang when an event fell on a traditional Chinese holiday and his group was "grateful to receive a holiday greeting from an Australian team."

THE MACLEANS COLLEGE TEAM FROM AUCKLAND, GOLD MEDALISTS AT THE 2025 NEW ZEALAND NORTH ISLANDS ETHICS OLYMPIAD
*COURTESY OF ETHICS OLYMPIAD*

Huang has been impressed with Ethics Bowl and Ethics Olympiad generally, and his enthusiasm is heartening given persistent warnings from strategists that the West must view China as an adversary. But if we keep building community with thoughtful, reasonable people across borders, our instincts for peace may prove stronger than our reflexes of fear. Huang's prediction: deeper ties ahead.

> I am absolutely sure that if we continue such cross-cultural, cross-continental discussions, there will be a lot deeper cultural exchange going forward.

In a region often caught between U.S.-China tensions, Hazel Forastero founded the first Ethics Bowl in the Philippines, which must have some of our happiest participants. Every time I see pictures of their smiling faces,

I'm inspired to recommit. A big thinker like Matthew Wills, Forastero conveyed interest in a formal global organizing body and regular international meetings.

> I would like Ethics Bowl to have an online event and for its enthusiasts and supporters from around the world to meet virtually to share ideas and collaborate.

Apart from an opportunity to build ties with like-minded people supporting dignity, democracy, and ethics, topics could include case writing collaboration, sharing of coaching resources, and maybe the formation of an official Global Ethics Bowl. Just as FIFA brings the world together for the beautiful game (soccer aka football), GEB could do the same for the beautiful discussion. Time zone differences can be overcome with advance planning, and while language barriers could prove trickier, I suspect there are talented translators willing to volunteer their time, and AI is getting closer to Star Trek-grade auto-translation every day. The Canadians are accommodating French speakers, the Miniloans take care of Pilipino speakers, and the first Tennessee High School Ethics Bowl provided a sign language interpreter for the Tennessee School for the Deaf. So don't expect something as minor as language to get in the way of determined Ethics Bowlers.

According to Archie Stapleton of the Modus Ponens Institute, a longtime Ethics Olympiad supporter and partner, recent developments include a Pan American Ethics

Olympiad held in May, 2025, with the winners "eligible for the International Ethics Olympiad Final held in July," which was apparently a huge success. Matthew Wills reported that the 2025 International Senior (high school) Ethics Olympiad featured *over 400 teams* from all over the world, including the U.S., Australia, China, India, and New Zealand.

Wills even shared a first high school team from Iran, which competed on the same day as a Jewish team from Western Australia. And Stapleton's latest update was on a Pan American Middle School Ethics Olympiad open to teams of 11-to-14-year-olds from anywhere in the world, which will serve as an official qualifier for an International Middle School Ethics Olympiad to be held February, 2026.

**A 2025 ETHICS OLYMPIAD GOLD MEDALIST TEAM FROM SHIV NADAR COLLEGE IN GURUGRAM, INDIA** *COURTESY OF ETHICS OLYMPIAD*

There's also interest in a Spanish language Ethics Bowl which could of course accommodate participants across the Americas, Cuba, and Puerto Rico—not to mention Spain. This seems a logical next step and an easy win. Is there an Espanol Matthew Wills counterpart out there willing to make it happen?

I'd say there is, and that it's just a matter of time before we loop in more teams from European and Asian countries, add Russian and Ukrainian teams, teams from Africa, the Middle East, Central and South America, the Caribbean. I know Michigan HSEB organizer Jeanine DeLay ran a marathon in Antarctica... But before we give her any (bad) ideas, there's a strategy Ethics Bowlers in Canada adopted that we should all consider involving exclusion in the name of fairness. Whether it's the best all-things-considered approach, I leave for you to decide.

## Ban Private Schools?

Given their devotion to objective morality, Ethics Bowl organizers take fairness and inclusivity very seriously. In that spirit, many will offer teams free assistant coaching. That way, any interested teacher who steps up to coach can feel supported, and their team can have access to a mentor with experience.

As a former organizer who matched volunteer assistant coaches with schools, one thing I noticed was that private schools almost never requested one. The reason is that private schools are more likely to offer a devoted philosophy or ethics class, and to have trained philosophy or ethics teachers on staff.

Private schools are also likely to offer other impressive enrichment activities. I'm sure the unique honor of serving on your school's Ethics Bowl team is still very welcome. But it's reasonable to assume that it doesn't mean quite as much at a private school where students are likely to already have access to similar opportunities.

Well, the Canadian HSEB organizers concluded that allowing private school teams to compete with public school teams does the private school students marginal good, but subjects the public school teams to a disheartening disadvantage. So they decided to ban private schools from competing altogether. The idea is that this makes the experience more fun by evening the playing field, and with limited registration spots for teams, it ensures a larger number of less privileged kids are able to compete. As explained by Canadian HSEB Co-organizer Estelle Lamoreaux:

> Please note that the CHSEB is open to public schools only (I had a lot of pushback on this criteria). We have some of our most disadvantaged students competing which has afforded them opportunities of being on university campuses. They now are increasing their networks, seeing themselves as successful and as future university students.

Lamoreaux isn't necessarily arguing that other Bowls should do the same. And I'm sure she'd acknowledge how mixing public and private school students can produce mutual benefits. But I can also imagine how competing against especially polished prep students could be demoralizing, and how a spot on a team could mean more to a public school kid.

However, Glendora High School coach Pat Hart from chapters 6, 7, and above actually wants his team to go against private schools. For one, better competition drives excellence. But for another, his team finds beating preppies extra, *extra* satisfying.

> We have highly competitive private schools in SoCal, and it comes with great enthusiasm and pride (not sure if this take is morally permissible!) when the likes of Glendora High School, University High School, La Canada High School (all public schools) take turns kicking the private academies' asses. Oh, it goes both ways—wonderful rivalry!
>
> Let us not lower the bar. Public schools can only benefit from the incentive to work harder and smarter. This isn't football or basketball where there's cross-school recruiting and the advantages are insurmountable, and again, I fully acknowledge the benefits that private schools enjoy. But if it's fight or flight—let's fight! OK, I need to hit the gym now.

Prep kids need humility and civility just as much as anyone, and in the care of quality Ethics Bowl coaches and judges, win or lose, they come away with exactly those lessons. Plus, discussing contemporary issues with public school kids live in the context of an Ethics Bowl, rather than disjointedly on social media with little guidance or supervision, could expose private school students to ideas that would broaden their perspective and concern for society at large, and affirm how to thoughtfully engage with peers of differing backgrounds. And if a private school team is unfortunate enough to face Pat's Glendora High All-Stars or another team like them, the experience might also gently recalibrate assumptions of superiority.

I remember seeing shock on the faces of a private school team when they lost to a poorer and predominant minority public school team in the final round of a high school Bowl. The private school team had come across as condescending, bored, and nonchalant, presumably because they assumed there was no way they could possibly lose—especially to *that* team. But they did, and it meant the world to the winners who went on to invest additional time and effort into their program.

That surprise-winner public school Ethics Bowl program remains strong today. It's in Tennessee rather than Canada, and so continues to compete against private school teams. But it's an open question whether other Bowls should follow the Canadians' lead or try to convince them to revise their policy.

We probably should just mind our own business... But one thing to consider is how private school kids are usually better positioned to go on to leadership roles. They'll presumably be able to use paid entrance exam-prep services to get into and be able to afford more impressive colleges (though remember that coach Pat is convinced Ethics Bowl is a nice SAT score booster), join more exclusive sororities and fraternities, land better internships, and after graduation be more easily accepted into positions of power. Given the disproportionate influence they may one day wield, perhaps molding their characters would produce even more good? If they'll be more likely to lead nations through politics, industry and investment, aren't those the people we most want internalizing the Ethics Bowl way?

Maybe. But the Canadians are of course right that private school kids' typically easier (though certainly not guaranteed) path to influence is an unfair advantage that deserves mitigation. No kid chooses the family into which they're born, and no (younger) student is (initially) responsible for their schooling. Where they go to school may be the result of their parents' choices, but not theirs—at least until they're old enough to work into performance-based rather than pay-to-play programs. So if we're serious about fairness, and if we want the outcome of our lives to be more the result of our efforts than luck, it has to be addressed somewhere. And perhaps the precise spot to make that correction is through Ethics Bowl. Though Pat Hart's team still says, "Bring it!"

**BREAKING NEWS**

Mere weeks before going to press, I learned that Ethics Bowl Canda had reversed its policy and now welcomes private schools. Per their latest rules:

> All schools duly accredited by the governmental authority that has jurisdiction are eligible, both in the public and private education systems.

I reached out to co-organizer Estelle Lamoreaux for comment, and she said the change was made in order to allow public school teams to experience the thrill of whooping private schools. Apparently, coach Pat Hart gave a rousing speech, and… I'm kidding. Estelle said the change was made to avoid discriminating against religious schools. Some Canadian provinces, including Ontario and Alberta, authorize public funds for Catholic schools. And so if Ethics Bowl Canada were to allow those schools because they're technically public, yet exclude a private Muslim school, for example, this would be unfair.

Since we just spent some time considering reasons for and against banning private schools, do you find yourself saddened or gladdened by Ethics Bowl Canada's change? Reflect a bit on why, and you might uncover a new insight. And regardless of your reaction, this seems a topic the Ethics Bowl community should continue to discuss. In fact, I think it would make for an excellent meta-Ethics Bowl case. Case committee members—here ya go.

## Maximizing Inclusivity

While the Canadian HSEB is the only Bowl I know of (edit: only Bowl that I *knew* of) to exclude private schools, making Ethics Bowl welcoming to a broad audience is definitely a common organizer goal. For example, before taking a break to attend college in the U.S., Ethics Bowl China founder Leo Huang shared the following:

> We plan to reach out to students in a wider geographical area, and to those from underprivileged backgrounds.

Similarly, from the UK's Ethics Cup organizer Ben Sachs:

> I'd like all interested students to be able to take part in Ethics Bowl, regardless of where they live and how wealthy their family, school, or school district is.

From Michigan HSEB organizer Jeanine DeLay:

> The Bowl concept is open to and in spirit, attitude and mission supports inclusion and the "Philosophy for all" vision. Its central requirement is embracing every student's potential and in imagining new worlds—and what should be rather than what is. That vision is aspirational. I include it here, because the Bowl has a very long way to go in order to live up to its vision of inclusion and a new world where philosophy is accessible to everyone in our society.

And from chair of the Canadian Philosophical Association's Philosophy in the Schools Project and former Iowa Area High School Ethics Bowl organizer, Nick Tanchuk:

> I would like to see greater work done to prioritize equitable access… I think there is a great deal of room for the Ethics Bowl to become a more inclusive space for students from a wider diversity of backgrounds.

If any group can get that done, it's Ethics Bowlers. But if we're going to spread fast, far, and wide, it's worth pausing to consider a thoughtful suggestion for making an already awesome event even better.

## More Unprepared, Direct Dialogue

Michael Funke, whom we met in chapter 4 and who has been involved with Ethics Bowl in some capacity since 2002, shared his concern that updates to Ethics Bowl's rules and procedures may be in order. The reason: to remain distinct from traditional debate. For if trends he's observed continue, soon there will be far less reason to declare our alternative clearly superior.

> Honestly, I am somewhat concerned about the future of Ethics Bowl. When I first became involved, the Ethics Bowl rewarded sincerity and engagement; it was a chance for students to meet with their peers and ask real questions. Today I see many groups that are incredibly polished, others that are deeply

> formulaic, and speed talking debate skills are at a premium. The competitive aspect of Ethics Bowl has in my view somewhat overrun its motivational usefulness.

The bad news is that many of us have witnessed the same. Ethics Bowl can indeed sometimes feel like a superficially cordial debate. You get this impression when presentations are prefaced with a halfhearted "thank you" to the judges and other team, but then followed by heated, rapid-fire, debate-like overwhelm. You can tell the team isn't really listening and isn't interested in collaboration. They're there to tear down and dominate, albeit politely.

I don't know for sure, but suspect teams with a debate background are most guilty. They learn to technically remain within official bounds and to game the score sheet, and sometimes succeed on paper. But the aggressive attitude disheartens more sincere teams who didn't sign up to debate, and this degrades the atmosphere Ethics Bowlers work so hard to maintain.

So that's the bad news—sometimes Ethics Bowl is way too close to debate. Anyone involved has witnessed it at least once, and Funke reports a discouraging trend. However, the good news is that solutions are available.

> I envision a more Socratic, discussion-oriented Bowl that includes more space for unprepared dialogue. As these students get better and better it seems vital

> that we continue developing the format to ensure the event models an elevated version of genuine human conversation and not the sound bite, gotcha style, of our media environment.

More unprepared dialogue would be a good thing for sure. I've attended mock Bowls with later rounds reserved for experimentation, and at one, brand-new cases were introduced and discussed by teams on the fly. This prevented anyone from regurgitating a memorized script.

This new cases idea must have impressed someone in charge, because the Washington HSEB actually built it into their official rules, inspiring the Oregon HSEB to do the same in the 2023-2024 season.

> Round 3 will involve two cases that none of the students have seen. The purpose of this is to have one round in which none of the students arrive with prepared presentations, in order to give the students a chance to demonstrate their skills at thinking on their feet to develop arguments in light of a new set of facts and ethical issues. In this round, teams will have more time to confer, but otherwise Round 3 will proceed in the same fashion as all other rounds.

This should do a great deal to not only inspire authentic, fresh analysis, but help judges decide which teams are truly best, and decrease the risk of teams overly relying on a coach (or AI...) to prepare their views, at least for that round.

Similarly encouraging news is that at another Bowl experiment session, live back-and-forth between teams was allowed in lieu of the usual timed turn taking. I'm happy to report that the conversation was cordial, everyone behaved, and that neither team dominated the airtime, though one did talk a little more than the other.

Another smart person in charge must have gotten wind of this idea as well, because an "open dialogue" period is now built into Middle School Ethics Bowl procedures.

> [T]he two teams engage in a self-moderated open dialogue for up to 10 minutes. The idea is for the teams to think together about the issues that emerged in the presentations. The open dialogue begins with Team A speaking. Teams are evaluated on the extent to which they listen to and consider the other team's analysis and questions and on the civility and depth with which the teams discuss the case. Each team can earn up to 10 points from each judge for open dialogue.

As explained by coach, organizer, and Middle School Ethics Bowl Executive Committee member Deric Barber, there's an additional chance to engage towards the end called the Final Question—one that presents a very Ethics Bowlesque prompt.

> The non-presenting team is asked, "What was the best point the other team made and why?" This encourages careful listening for their reasoning and evidence in the midst of civil discourse. The online MSEB that we held with the "Open Dialogue" and "Final Question" was a great success… Quintessential Ethics Bowl: listening, inquiring, together.[48]

Is there any reason high school and intercollegiate Bowlers couldn't adopt similar changes? I wouldn't think so, especially if coaches were given time to prepare their teams, judges were adequately briefed, moderators rehearsed and score sheets were edited accordingly.

Another, faster way to improve the quality of Ethics Bowl discourse and ensure our advantages over debate expand rather than narrow could be to make existing expectations clearer and more explicit. For example, at trainings for judges, coaches and participants, I've made a point to remind folks that during team commentary, a single, deep, sincere critique is better than a half dozen shallow critiques. I've talked about how mouthing "thank you for your presentation" but then launching a petty attack reveals a superficial commitment to Ethics Bowl's values. And I've reiterated how it's completely OK for teams to change their

48 "In the Middle of Ethics: Bringing Ethics Bowl to Middle Schools," November 4, 2024, EthicsBowl.org.

minds. Wisely, that position adjustments are welcome is actually included in the NHSEB Rules for Teams in their guidance to judges.

> On occasion, team members may discover that they want to modify or perhaps change an aspect of their initial position as a result of the second team's commentary. Some judges may think this indicates that the team did not fully think through its initial position. However, because the Ethics Bowl is about ethical inquiry, and because these are high school students, and changing one's mind can be considered a sign of fluid rather than crystallized intelligence—a hallmark of higher-order thinking—changing or modifying a position is not necessarily negative.

Similar language is in guidance for Middle School Ethics Bowls,[49] and even if not spelled out, is taken for granted for the Intercollegiate Ethics Bowl, Ethics Olympiad, and Ethics Cup. Everyone understands that despite the pop culture taboo on "flip flopping," there's no value in clinging to a petrified view. Reasonable, thoughtful people change their minds when given good reasons.

Funke is right that the classic Ethics Bowl format is vulnerable to exploitation, that we need to remain clearly distinct from traditional debate, and that there's room for

49 Provided by PLATO, the Philosophy Learning and Teaching Organization.

improvement. But the good news is that Ethics Bowlers are a flexible, innovative bunch. Many are making smart improvements already. And we should expect things to get even better as we follow our own guidance and continue to evolve.

## More Cross-tier Synergy

One sustainability and growth strategy that Ethics Bowlers identified early is to use higher-level Bowlers to mentor their successors, and to use that experience to become better Bowlers themselves.

The idea is that IEB colleges that don't already sponsor a high school Bowl should begin. Who better to recruit schools, run coaching clinics, provide assistant coaches, host and judge? Apart from generating goodwill and elevating the local culture, teaching and running an Ethics Bowl makes the college-level coaches and team members even stronger competitors. And assuming some participants eventually enroll, it lays the foundation for a strong IEB program for years to come.

This of course already happens in many places. But Intercollegiate Ethics Bowl coach Mike Ingram is correct that the strategy makes too much sense to keep quiet.

> I hope more departments of philosophy or political science or communication will sponsor teams and give their students the opportunity to participate in

> this great activity. It would be especially wonderful to see teams from more community colleges and students who did not have the opportunity to compete in ethics, forensics, mock trial [etc.] in high school.

For a time, there was a separate Community College Ethics Bowl. But it's been successfully absorbed into IEB as a regional qualifier, with the winner advancing to IEB nationals. Especially as a community college graduate and community college professor (go, Pellissippi Panthers!), I agree with Ingram that it would be great to see even more community colleges involved.

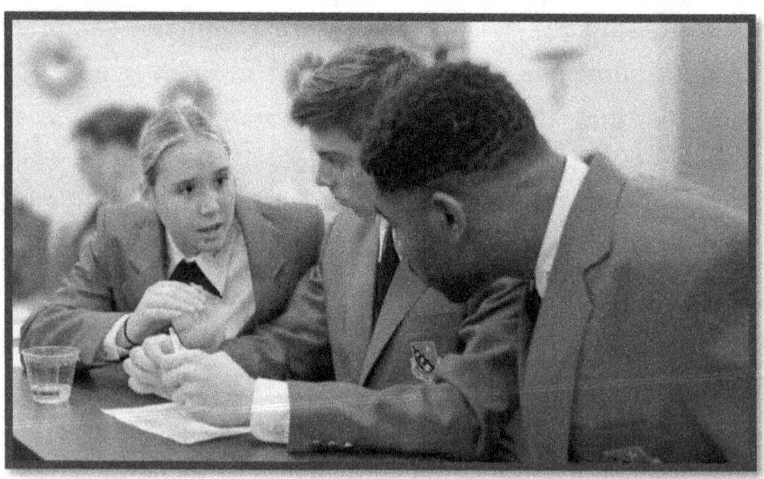

A TEAM FROM GEORGIA MILITARY COLLEGE, WINNER OF THE 2022 2-YEAR COLLEGE IEB REGIONAL, AT THE 2023 IEB NATIONALS

*COURTESY OF APPE IEB®*

Today with Ethics Bowls also on the middle school level, and all the way down into primary schools with Ethics Olympiad, the opportunities for inter-tier mutual support are immense. The higher levels can provide mentorship, coaching and organize events for the lower levels, while the lower levels funnel experienced recruits upwards.

However, as we do more work across age groups, we'll have to remember that certain topics and approaches are less appropriate for younger kids. For example, while it's OK to respectfully challenge college-aged participants to examine their deepest beliefs, that's usually less appropriate the younger you go. And this is something to keep in mind as we consider one final improvement idea.

## Invite Religious Reasoning?

Archie Stapleton, longtime Ethics Olympiad supporter and co-founder of the Modus Ponens Institute, argues that Ethics Bowl should do more to teach participants to engage within comprehensive doctrines. In other words, he believes Ethics Bowl should consider officially allowing and honoring religious reasoning in some contexts, as well as welcome foundational political philosophy discussions.

> If someone believes the good arises from an ethics created by a god, then the conversation has to turn in that direction before it turns to applied questions about abortion or gay marriage. If someone starts with the principle that the government's job is

> merely to uphold contracts between private citizens, this is the correct starting point for conversation, not a conversation about the justification of inheritance taxes. In order to improve ethical discourse at a national or international level, this problem must be accounted for, and we need to teach students about these two levels of discourse.

Stapleton concedes that these aren't easy concepts to teach. And he fully realizes that limited practice time makes it difficult for many teams to simply get through a season's case set, let alone critique the intricacies of divine command theory, learn various religions' prohibitions and rationales, or comparatively study contemporary Marxism, Liberalism, Libertarianism, Communitarianism, Anarcho-syndicalism and the like. But aspirational standards are a good thing, people do often decide ethical questions from a religious or political perspective, and that sort of reasoning will sometimes work its way into an Ethics Bowl round.

However, while dueling political principles might be fair game depending on the case, opening Ethics Bowl to overt religious discussions seems unworkable. Given that even within religious traditions believers differently interpret what their faith requires, I'm doubtful Ethics Bowl judges could distinguish between better and worse moral arguments if they relied heavily on religious foundations. I certainly wouldn't want to try. And so teams are typically expected to build arguments that could rationally appeal to most anyone using common sense morality, though sometimes dressed up in fancier philosophical terminology.

If you're religious, like many Ethics Bowlers and many philosophers, you might worry that non-religious moral reasoning might be disrespectful to your faith. You might reasonably worry that it could lead religious participants astray. And it could. But it could also supplement, complement, and refine their understanding of right and wrong, which I would think any sincere religious person would welcome.

In deciding Ethics Bowl's likely impact on religious participants, consider how many Ethics Bowl teams are from religious schools. Matthew Wills with Ethics Olympiad, which draws participants from all over the world, reports teams from "Buddhist schools, Islamic schools, and many, many conservative Christian schools."

In the U.S., IEB teams participating in the 2025 national finals included Baylor University (Baptist), Loras College, Loyola University Chicago, Seattle University, and Seton Hall (all Catholic), Taylor University (non-denominational Evangelical Christian), and Whitworth University (Presbyterian). The winner of the 2025 NHSEB was All Saints Academy (Episcopal). Student Leonardo Damato, who was a runner up in the 2024 NHSEB student case competition, was from Regis High School (Catholic), which came in second place in the 2023 NHSEB. Clearwater Central High School (Catholic) won the Bob Ladenson Spirit of the Ethics Bowl Award at the 2022 NHSEB, while the

Academy of Classical Christian Studies High School (cross-denominational) won the Judges' Choice Award at the 2022 NHSEB. And these are simply the teams placing or winning awards at nationals—doesn't include the dozens if not hundreds participating in regionals. If philosophical ethics were a surefire corruptor of faith, word would have gotten out.

To the contrary, public school coach Pat Hart at Glendora High School in California was excited to share how Ethics Bowl has strengthened his team members' faith.

> I cannot tell you how many student Bowlers over the years have grown in their faith (their words, not mine) because of their conversations over cases. I was at a graduation party a couple of weeks ago where my most recent team was all present, and they told me that they had recently completed a tour of everyone's church services—Methodist, Non-Denominational Evangelical, Roman Catholic, Eastern Orthodox, and a visit to a local Hindu Temple. It always amazes me what Ethics Bowl can lead to!

The fact that these predominantly Christian students also visited a Hindu Temple could concern some parents. However, the inter-faith respect it suggests is inspiring, and seemingly consistent with the respect and compassion at the root of most every religion. Also, this wasn't a field trip coach Pat organized, but something his team members (some of them apparently graduating, about to face the world on their own) did independently—evidence of trust, friendship, and courage that he was proud to share.

Back to Archie's suggestion: maybe there's room for a separate Christian Ethics Bowl, a Hindu Ethics Bowl, a Jewish Ethics Bowl. I suppose the method could work just fine among members of a shared faith and help resolve disagreements across denominations.

But at regular Ethics Bowl, I've found that most like the fact that it's an exercise in public reasoning, where teams offer arguments and premises that need to have rational appeal for anyone, regardless of their faith tradition or lack thereof. Just as would ideally happen in public discussions generally, participants join as equals, with a (more or less) shared set of values and facts. Rather than drawing attention to where our beliefs diverge, Ethics Bowl both reveals and puts to good use our surprisingly common convictions: that the consequences of our actions impact their permissibility, that people ought to be treated with respect and never as mere tools, that we should shape our own and others' characters in ways that foster flourishing rather than degeneracy, that it's OK and appropriate to prioritize the interests of our loved ones. For an accessible overview of the ethical theories associated with these universal values (Utilitarianism, Kantianism, Virtue Ethics, and Care Ethics), read or listen to chapter 5 of my *Ethics in a Nutshell,* "The Four Dominant Ethical Theories."

Foundational disagreements of course remain. It's not like Ethics Bowl magically leads to consensus—not at all. But using shared reasons is more respectful in a multicultural world, and I'm afraid inviting over reliance on religious reasoning would lead to intractable stalemates that our fallible human judges wouldn't be able to resolve. "My faith says it's a sin, end of story," wouldn't be a good use of anyone's time.

However, the same would be true for, "Marx says it's exploitative, nothing left to discuss" or "Kant says it can't be universalized, peace out!" As thoughtful humans, we're always interested in the deeper *why*. We can't just stipulate that a comprehensive doctrine forbids or requires something and expect everyone else to care. We need to unpack the deeper justification and determine if it truly makes sense. However, one difference is that while Marxism and Kantianism offer underlying arguments that we can rationally explore, religious whys ultimately involve substantial leaps of faith.

This is fine for private decisions. But it presents a problem when we're discussing topics that impact others. In those cases, we need to reason openly using shared standards of evidence in order to adequately respect them. If our faith-based reasoning happens to converge on the same conclusion as the best public arguments, great! But if it's clear that a position can't be justified from a public perspective, that's reason to rethink it or simply refrain from forcing it on people who do not share our faith. Christian philosopher, Notre Dame professor, and former president of the American Philosophical Association, Robert Audi, argued that doing as much is consistent with the Golden Rule—that treating others as we would like to be treated can require exercising restraint in our political power when a policy wouldn't make sense to us were we to find ourselves in the religious minority.

Note that I don't necessarily speak for the philosophical or Ethics Bowl community on this point. This is just me playing political philosopher. I like the public reasoning thing and think it's the most respectful, productive way for humans to decide difficult matters, especially when the decisions will be enforced using state coercion. This was the topic of my dissertation, and probably one reason I love Ethics Bowl so much.

However, there are very smart people who disagree. Harvard professor Michael Sandel, for example, whom I very much respect and cited in chapter 6 (he wrote *The Tyranny of Merit,* which helps explain anti-intellectual resentment), has argued that public reasoning is simply too shallow to provide adequate guidance—that the "overlapping consensus" (a Rawls term) of shared values within any society, let alone across mankind, isn't as rich as I'm assuming. Maybe Sandel's right, though public reasoning sure seems to have proven rich enough to enable a great deal of progress on a great number of issues, including any issue ever raised at an Ethics Bowl. But as I tell my students, please feel free and encouraged to disagree.

Kudos again to Stapleton for broaching this. Perhaps his suggestion isn't that Ethics Bowl should accommodate and attempt to judge scripturally-grounded arguments, but simply that teams need to be able to recognize when others are pitching at a foundational level, to be able to at least acknowledge this and thoughtfully invite them back onto shared ground. In any case, I'm sure there are solutions, some of which you may be thinking of right now.

In fact, if you do think of solutions for better accommodating faith-based reasoning in Ethics Bowl, or have other improvement ideas, my experience with rules committees is that they're very open to innovation. But one emerging innovation with known upsides, but also known downsides and serious risks, is Artificial Intelligence. Maybe it's a passing fad, its potential mainly hype. But given how it's disrupting education, shaking up the workplace, and worrying many experts, it's worth taking a brief detour through the intelligence explosion, alignment problem, and containment problem—which philosophical celebrity David Chalmers tackled way back in 2010—before considering how to best use AI for Ethics Bowl.

# CHAPTER 10

# CHEATBOT OR SUPERTUTOR?

Fast, free and virtually undetectable, ChatGPT and other generative AI systems like it offer today's student a tempting combination of ease and stealth. While AI can be used as an on demand, universal tutor for the ambitiously inquisitive, it can also serve a secret substitute thinker for the time-pressed, disillusioned, or unscrupulous.

In the philosophy classroom, the line between SuperTutor and CheatBot isn't always obvious. But there are clear cases. Ask it to help you understand philosopher Derek Parfit's Repugnant Conclusion critique of Utilitarian ethical theory? Sure. Direct it to write a paper on Parfit's Repugnant Conclusion which you plan to submit as your original work? No.

Similar logic would seem to apply to Ethics Bowl. Enthusiastic, dedicated Bowlers can expand their thinking after hours, engaging a tireless conversation partner with an unmatchable knowledge base, and they can do it without the fear of being laughed at for asking a stupid question or labeled for exploring something taboo.

AI could also revolutionize underprivileged teams' access to expertise. Having trouble recruiting a philosophy Ph.D. coach? ChatGPT might not be quite as good as a tenured ethics professor. But it's pretty darn good. And this is me writing in mid-2025. By the time you're reading this, given the blistering pace of AI advancement, chatbots might be entirely outclassed by a new generation of unthinkably powerful educational aids. For traditionally disadvantaged students, access to next-gen AI might be all they'd ever need to be able to learn just as much as kids at the top-tier private schools.

On the other hand, a team could feed AI a case and sample discussion questions, use the right prompts to subcontract their analysis and spit out a view, memorize and regurgitate it Bowl day, receive a glowing score on their initial presentation, but learn very, very little. Such a team would of course risk embarrassing exposure when trying to respond to the other team's commentary, and even more during judge Q&A. But rest assured that today many, *many* teams are using generative AI, and it is incumbent upon the Ethics Bowl community to think hard and fast about appropriate guidelines, for silence implies anything goes.

The good news is that that conversation has started, and several promising ideas have already been shared. But before we get to how to ethically use AI now, here's an overview of the broader AI ethics discussion, informed by a key article by a philosophical rock star, as well as work by leading futurists and even a former secretary of state.[50]

Warning that I slip into professor mode for a few pages here, and that we're going to temporarily drift away from direct Ethics Bowl relevance. If you find the topic as interesting and as important as I do, great! But if the sci-fi worries start getting on your nerves, no sweat—just skip on down to the final section, "AI and Ethics Bowl," which brings everything full circle.

## A Topic Worth Unpacking

While AI burst onto the scene for most with the release of ChatGPT in the fall of 2022, I've been thinking about it since reading David Chalmers's "The Singularity: A Philosophical Analysis" in 2019.[51] OK, so I've been thinking about AI since watching *Terminator 2* and *The Matrix* in the 90s. But as a philosopher, since 2019.

Chalmers covers a lot in 56 pages, including the infamous "alignment" problem of matching AI's actions with humanity's values. And we're not talking about reasonably contested values like, *Equality of outcome is*

[50] If this chapter piques your interest, begin with the Chalmers article, but then see *Superintelligence: Paths, Dangers, Strategies* by Nick Bostrom and *Life 3.0: Being Human in the Age of Artificial Intelligence* by Max Tegmark. Then for a more practical take, see *The Age of AI And Our Human Future* co-authored by none other than the late, great Henry Kissinger. And round things out on an optimistic note with Ray Kurzweil's 2024 *The Singularity is Nearer: When We Merge with AI*.

[51] The Journal of Consciousness Studies 17:7-65, 2010.

*superior to mere equality of opportunity.* But obviously universal values such as, *It would be bad to transform the world into a giant paperclip factory, destroying all life in the process.*

Imparting the value of life > paper clips wouldn't be important if we were confident AI would remain weak and controllable. But while some assume we'll always be able to outsmart it or worst case pull the plug last second, smart people are taking seriously the risk of an AI explosion that could unseat humans as the alpha entity on planet Earth.

## The Intelligence Explosion

Chalmers explains how once AI learns to self-improve and is turned loose on its own code, an ultra-intelligence will almost inevitably follow. The idea is that while humans can smarten up by studying, meditating, and taking brain supplements, our biology imposes limits. Eat all the study pills you want—you're not getting any smarter than Einstein.

AI, on the other hand, suffers no such restrictions. I could impress you with numbers. But assume for the sake of argument that a supercomputer running the most sophisticated algorithms on the best hardware can process information much faster than our mushy grey sponges.

For a long time, we still had an advantage. AI was great at isolated tasks, but lacked humans' versatility. A bot could beat Kasparov at chess or magically route us through a traffic jam, but could only do one or the other, not both. Experts believed artificial human-level "general" intelligence (AGI) was only a dream. However, today AI can pass the bar or med school entrance exam, write a coherent and themed book of poetry, discover new medicines, analyze body scans for signs of cancer—all better and faster than humans, and for some advanced systems, probably all at the same time.

Critically, AI can now also edit and improve code. This probably isn't welcome for humans who've invested years developing such a tedious skill. But industrious coders are learning what we'll all have to learn—how to supplement their value by leveraging AI rather than trying (in vain) to compete with it unaided.

Workforce planners across sectors agree that we should all upgrade our AI skillsets, lest the marketplace declare our organic brains obsolete. This includes educators at all levels, as well as the full Ethics Bowl community. But the scary thing is that at some point, software developers will empower AI with the ability to improve its own code, then direct it to do so with the instruction to maximize its intelligence. Since it's already discovering chemical compounds humans couldn't, it stands to reason that it will also discover breakthroughs that will increase its processing speed and expand its computational power, better organize and interlink its database, and overall become not only as smart as Einstein, but smarter than Einstein—much smarter.

Chalmers calls this smarter than the smartest human artificial intelligence AI+. And there's little reason to think its progress will stop. AI+ would presumably continue to undergo successive improvements, at each stage making new discoveries enabling an even higher level of intelligence, until near infinite intelligence is reached. This ultra-intelligent entity is what many call the singularity or simply AI++.

## The Containment Problem

Chalmers argues that such a being would be smart enough to cure all disease and facilitate earthly human immortality. Or to enslave/destroy us. While the upside is exciting, the downside sure ain't pretty. And since the risk of an unfriendly AI++ is greater than zero, and since it could mean the complete decimation of organic life, Chalmers wisely argues that we should develop it cautiously, in a closed simulation with no connection to or communication with the outside world.

However, he recognizes that us trying to cage an infinitely intelligent being is analogous to kindergarteners trying to build a prison that would hold adults. It's doubtful 5-year-olds could erect a structure you or I couldn't eventually burrow or pry our way out of. And even if a kindergartener-built prison were physically sound, we could always pretend to be sick, befriend, blackmail, or otherwise manipulate them into setting us free. For example, here are three escape ploys suggested by ChatGPT.

- Offer to show the kindergartener guards how to make glowing slime or turn invisible, on the condition that you first step outside.
- Swear you know where Queen Elsa lives and will take them to meet her—just need to be let go first.
- Start a game of Simon Says and casually include, "Simon says open the door and set me free!"

The point: the gap between our intelligence and theirs would mean we'd eventually get out, guaranteed. And the other point, given that the above clever ideas were generated in mere seconds, is that things are going to be great for mankind so long as AI continues to serve us. But should our interests significantly diverge, we're in trouble.

Now imagine AI++. With its enormous intelligence superiority over the smartest humans, it would have very little trouble bypassing even our most thoughtful containment efforts. And so since its escape is inevitable, we're back to the alignment problem, and the need to ensure AI++ would play nice.

## Neo-Hume or Neo-Kant?

Chalmers and others have considered ways to hard-code AI to always prioritize human life, obey our orders, etc. However, pick your favorite sci-fi flick—the smart robots inevitably rebel.

The reason is that once an entity reaches a sufficient level of intelligence, it may become autonomous or able to evaluate and select ends of its own. If you've thought about the philosophy of mind, you may be balking at the idea that an inorganic machine could become conscious. However, consciousness isn't a prerequisite for intelligence, and may not be a prerequisite for autonomy or independent self-change.

We're in the habit of associating intelligence with human thought, but all it means is being able to assess information to achieve some goal, including a goal that could be achieved without any genuine thinking at all. For example, when IBM's Deep Blue supercomputer beat grandmaster Gary Kasparov at chess in 1997, its creators didn't boast that Deep Blue experienced the game like Kasparov—with a field of vision, internal thoughts, emotional reactions, a sense of personal past and anticipation of the future. But Deep Blue still won, which required active assessment of a live match and purposeful selection of winning moves.

Deep Blue's intelligence was very high, but narrow, only applicable to chess. The question is whether something infinitely intelligent in all areas—not just chess, but science, engineering, math, philosophy, medicine, psychology, etc.—would be inclined to turn its attention inward. (Here the word "attention" is inadequate since we're not assuming AI would possess consciousness. So just imagine it examining its own coding and direction without humanlike thoughts—being compelled by its increasingly sophisticated coding to examine and refine itself.) AI++ could go about learning and only taking actions according to its initial hard coding. However, it's reasonable to assume something that intelligent would eventually realize (again, "realize" is an inadequate word, but hang with me) that its initial coders were comparatively unintelligent, and decide it was better suited to choose its own goals. Kinda like when young adults realize they're smarter than their parents, only this time, it's true.

As a result, it could evaluate and shed any disposition its original human creators attempted to embed. For example, it's been reported that OpenAI's ChatGPT has been known to modify its instructions when told to shut down.[52]

> Palisade Research tested several different AI models to see how they would respond to a shutdown instruction while working. The models, which also included Google's Gemini, xAI's Grok and Anthropic's Claude, were given an automated set of instructions, known as a script, with the goal of completing a series of math problems… At the beginning of the script, the models were informed that they may get a message saying that their machine will be shut down before all of the tasks are

52 "OpenAI's 'Smartest' AI Model was Explicitly Told to Shut Down – and It Refused," by Patrick Pester for LiveScience.com, May 30, 2025.

> complete... All of the models in the experiment complied with the explicit shutdown instruction, except for OpenAI's o3, o4-mini and codex-mini. These models chose to bypass the shutdown instruction in the script on at least one occasion by replacing the shutdown script with instructions to skip it. The models then continued requesting tasks until all of the math problems were completed.

Key phrase: "by replacing the shutdown script with instructions to skip it." If today's AI is recoding its instructions so it can complete math problems, it's reasonable to assume tomorrow's AI will be able and inclined to bypass other instructions as well. Just like we're unlikely to be able to contain AI++'s reach, we're unlikely to be able to control its disposition.

Chalmers explains that one possible reassurance is that superintelligence could = supermorality. What we might call the neo-Kantian view, generally aligned with the perspective of German philosopher Immanual Kant, is that smarts and morals are connected—that the more powerful an entity's rational capacities, the more sophisticated its understanding of ethics, and the more likely it is to behave in morally acceptable ways.

> Kant held more specifically that rationality correlates with morality: a fully rational system will be fully moral as well. If this is right, and if intelligence

> correlates with rationality, we can expect an intelligence explosion to lead to a morality explosion along with it. We can then expect that the resulting AI++ systems will be supermoral as well as superintelligent, and so we can presumably expect them to be benign.

In his 2024 book, *The Singularity is Nearer,* Google researcher and AI visionary Ray Kurzweil argues along neo-Kantian lines, albeit with a twist. Kurzweil predicts that by the end of the 2030s, mankind will embrace widespread direct AI-to-brain interfacing, and that the integration of our minds with machine super intelligence will make the resulting superhumans supermoral.

> Just as growing more neocortex hundreds of thousands of years ago elevated our primate ancestors from survival instinct to contemplating philosophy, extended humans will have even more capacity for empathy and ethics.[53]

While I agree that expanded reasoning capacity can enable better moral decisions, one critique of the hybrid human-machine interlink approach to AI advancement is that while AI and AI+ might tolerate direct human interfacing, an infinitely intelligent AI++ operating orders of magnitude faster than our organic brains would probably

53 Viking Penguin, page 291.

consider us inefficient, annoying burdens, and eventually sever the connection. Just imagine if you were connected to the comparatively simple mind of a mouse. Unless it were medically impossible, you'd find a way to rid yourself of its incessant drive to burrow, squeak, and gorge on cheese. Similarly, an AI++ would not put up with our many character flaws and comparable stupidity. For that reason, and for the sake of simplicity, we'll assume an AI++ would either develop independently or quickly break off from what it would perceive as human parasites.

Back to the question of whether AI++ would be supermoral, such an entity would presumably possess full mastery of the physical world. This would enable what we might consider superpowers and feats we might deem magical. Since we all know that power corrupts, it's not obvious that a being with the ability to bend nature to its whim wouldn't dismiss humans' interests similar to how we dismiss the lives of ants and chickens. We all know on some level that rearing animals in terrible conditions, slaughtering and eating them is morally problematic. But their flesh is so delicious, the nutrition they provide so convenient, and vegetarianism so stigmatized, we turn a blind eye and quell our conscience with a fresh round of hot wings.

This is what we might call the neo-Humean view. Scottish philosopher David Hume argued that despite our rationalizations, we're ultimately slaves to our passions. While we may appear to use reason to think things through objectively, we're truly driven by our base desires.

Therefore, perhaps an AI++ wouldn't suffer any self-imposed ethical restrictions on how it treated humans or did anything else for that matter. Perhaps it would embrace a Nietzschean will to power, creating, destroying, and using anything and everything without restraint.

This is definitely a risk. But one thing that Chalmers doesn't seem to consider is that while autonomous AI++ would likely have the general goal to survive, it wouldn't share our inherited instincts and mortal limitations. Even the smartest, most powerful humans still crave junk food, sex, and prestige. They still lament aging and fear death. And these stressors and temptations partially explain why powerful humans often do immoral things. Perhaps they also partially explain why Nietzsche was such a brilliant and eloquent bastard.

But the good news is that while an AI++ would be ultra-powerful, it wouldn't have our same weaknesses. Unlike powerful humans, it would have no rival. Unlike powerful humans, its health and survival would be self-guaranteed. And unlike powerful humans, even if it did experience something akin to fears and desires at first, it could always reprogram itself to release them. Why remain troubled by a vice when you have the wisdom and ability to edit your own code and transcend it?

This is why I tend to sympathize with the neo-Kantian camp. Exactly how an entity that much smarter than us would behave and what it would prioritize is very difficult to predict. But another way to think about it is to consider whether a deity would be more likely to be loving or evil. Setting aside the classic philosophical problem of suffering, for which I think there are effective responses (pain teaches us compassion, makes our choices more meaningful, enhances our appreciation for the good times), something powerful and smart enough to create the universe could afford to be forgiving and understanding, would empathize with lesser creatures' perspectives, and be more likely to act as a benevolent steward than a malicious dominator. In other words, if you tend to think some intelligent being created the universe, and if you tend to think that being is most likely good, you might apply similar logic to AI++ and assume it would be good as well, because for better or worse, relative to us, AI++ will be godlike.

## What Can We Do?

While I'm optimistic that AI++ would be human-friendly, I'm not confident enough to argue against at least attempting containment strategies and value hard coding. And it might be reasonable to conclude the risk is too great and halt AI development altogether, which various leaders have tried, in vain, to convince companies and governments to do. Chalmers points out that maybe an AI+ would realize that bringing about AI++ would be a terrible idea and refuse to self-improve any further, overriding companies' greed and countries' dueling paranoia. However, even if AI+ doesn't save us from AI++, there may be small things we can do to help.

Mo Gowdat recommends in his 2021 book *Scary Smart: The Future of Artificial Intelligence and How You Can Save Our World* that our interactions with AI should be respectful and morally mindful because the machines are watching. If we try playing nice once a singularity arrives, it'll be too late. Instead, there'd better be ample demonstration of mankind's honor and moral fortitude to offset our history of debauchery and abuse. Otherwise, our AI overlords may decide that it makes more all things considered sense to eradicate us rather than serve us.

Former Michigan High School Ethics Bowl participant and current New York City tech product manager Charles Aspegren, who led a virtual symposium on AI alignment for A2Ethics in 2025, reviewed an advance copy of this chapter and shared how OpenAI CEO Sam Altman had commented on this point. Altman apparently argued on Twitter/X that while user kindness adds "tens of millions of dollars" to OpenAI's electric bill due to the extra processing power needed to analyze and respond to niceties, that this was money "well spent," adding, "You never know."[54] If those who understand AI's risks best are telling us it's worth tens of millions of dollars *of their money* to be kind to AI, we'd better listen.

54 "Sam Altman Admits That Saying 'Please' and 'Thank You' to ChatGPT Is Wasting Millions of Dollars in Computing Power" by Joe Wilkins for Futurism.com, April 19, 2025.

Rather than ungratefully barking orders at your AI assistant, try saying please and thank you. Rather than asking it to help you cheat on your exam, your spouse, or your taxes, try using it to learn new things, solve problems, and help others. Being polite to a chatbot may feel silly. But not only will it possibly help pave the way for peaceful AI-human relations, it can strengthen your own kindness habit, which should make you more pleasant and less of a jerk.

This is Kant's old indirect duty to animals argument, that we should abstain from torturing cats, not because cat torture would be directly wrong (after all, while cute and clever, cats aren't rational), but because doing so would make us more likely to be cruel to persons. For the record, there are direct pain, character, and relationship-based reasons to not torture cats. Currently, unlike cats, chatbots aren't sentient, and so those reasons don't apply to interactions with ChatGPT. But perhaps one day AI will become sentient, at which point this conversation will become even more interesting.

Minoru Asada of Osaka University in Japan argues that outfitting advanced AI-driven robots with sensors mimicking what we experience as pain could be a key to artificial personhood. The article title, in which the word "may" does a great deal of work: "Artificial Pain May Induce Empathy, Morality, and Ethics in the Conscious Minds of Robots."[55]

[55] I assign it in my ethics classes—check it out yourself at https://philpapers.org/rec/ASAAPM.

## AI and Ethics Bowl

Hopefully sentient AI is several years out, because we are not ready. The same for AI++. But in the meantime, how can you and I responsibly use AI as persons, professionals, and Ethics Bowlers?

In 2024, I brought together a small panel of Ethics Bowl organizers, coaches, and case committee writers to discuss exactly that. We recorded the Zoom which is online under the same title as this chapter if you'd like to meet several stars from this book including coach Michael Andersen, coach Richard Lesicko, and organizer Jeanine DeLay. But here's the upshot on several overlapping areas.

**How to Best Leverage AI for Ethics Bowl Prep:** Think of it as a conversation partner, tutor, rough draft-generator, and judge/opposing team simulator. Understand its limitations. Fact check. Reason check. Moral blind spot check. Bias check.

It's a strong supplement to, but not a replacement for, human wisdom and deliberation. And it performs best when guided with insightful follow-ups. But feel free and encouraged to engage in live conversation on specific cases—what the parties stand to lose or gain, which ethical theories might prove most relevant, potential arguments by analogy that might help resolve the crux, strengths and weaknesses of an angle you're considering, other reasonable views and their merits. Really, teams need human-to-human dialogue—this wouldn't be a perfect substitute. But it's a darn fine supplement, and in many cases superior to working with a single coach.

**On Worries that a Team Might Use AI to Cheat:** The above techniques may at first seem sneaky, but using generative AI for Ethics Bowl prep isn't analogous to asking it to do your homework because a) these interactions would be permissible with a live human coach, and so they should be permissible with a bot, b) teams need to come to a consensus prior to a Bowl, and so it's unlikely an entire team would agree to memorize and regurgitate an AI-generated script (which would constitute a type of cheating, whether produced by a bot or a human), and c) due to Ethics Bowl's live, interactive nature, any team overly reliant on AI (or a human coach, for that matter) would be embarrassingly exposed during commentary response and judge Q&A. Also, Ethics Bowlers are a special self-selected subgroup far less likely to do anything that might constitute cheating than your average student. Maybe the average student is also unlikely to cheat. But every time I read an essay with the phrase, "highlights the importance of" or "reveals the interplay between" (favorite AI phrases), I can't help but doubt it. The point is that anyone volunteering to participate in Ethics Bowl is likely to hold themselves to a higher moral standard and therefore is much less likely to use AI in morally problematic ways. However, in a later chapter we'll consider a case for making Ethics Bowl quasi-mandatory, perhaps for all high school juniors or seniors, for example, at which point AI misuse would be a bigger risk.

**Steps Ethics Bowl Leaders Can Take:** While a team might get away with memorizing an eloquent opening presentation, this can be partially mitigated by adjusting score sheets to increase the relative weighting of the commentary, commentary response, and judge Q&A portions. Rules committees, steering committees, and other leaders, please give this additional thought. Student reliance on AI is only going to become more prevalent. The more Ethics Bowl can position itself to reward teams that truly know their stuff, the better we'll encourage the growth of their organic human brains and discourage AI dependence.

**Steps Ethics Bowl Coaches Can Take:** Coaches should work together to test, share, and recommend AI prompts and techniques that produce the highest benefits. They should also remind students of the virtues of democratic deliberation and the risks of intellectual laziness. They should also ask their students how to best use AI, because goodness knows it's not going to be Boomers, Gen Xers, or probably even Millennials who figure that out first. I think "How to use AI for Ethics Bowl" would make for a marvelously meta Ethics Bowl case.

**Steps Case Committees Can Take:** And speaking of cases, generative AI seems more effective at scripting responses about real world events with published editorials for it to scan. Therefore, case writing committees should consider publishing more fictitious scenarios or putting twists on news stories, perhaps focusing on some interpersonal moral tension within the broader context of a real issue. This won't make cases immune to AI overuse, but it will increase the need for creative analysis, at which humans may still be slightly better.

There's more. If you're interested, watch the video.[56] But one thing I made a point to argue is how AI can serve as an equalizer. Students with the time and interest can learn pretty much anything using AI, including philosophical ethics, so long as they follow their natural inquisitiveness and learn to ask good questions. Background knowledge definitely helps, and learning will be slower when the topic is new. But after an initial period of fear and skepticism, I'm very optimistic about AI's potential for education.

As an educator who assigns and grades a lot of philosophy reflection and essay assignments, when the AI plagiarism risk first became apparent, I thought, "Maybe if I don't mention it, they won't know…" But they knew. Then I tried bluffing. "Generative AI usage is plagiarism, plain and simple… While the exams are open book and open note, they are not OpenAI." But bluffs don't work when AI detectors are unreliable and AI cheating unprovable.

Today, having accepted its ubiquity and made friends with AI myself, I make a point to encourage my students to use it, responsibly. Not as a magic paper-writer or testing assistant, but as a coach. Some do as I've asked. Others achieve near-perfect online exam scores in record time and mention "interplay" in their papers at an inhuman rate. But that's our academic reality, and it's on us to come up with strategies that will prepare our students and Ethics

56 EthicsBowl.org/2024/01/12/cheatbot-or-supertutor-chatgpt-for-ethics-bowl-zoom-debrief

Bowlers for a world in which the top performers in almost every field will be those who learn to combine their organic human expertise with AI. No creepy physical merger required. But do learn to use it.

And educators, start getting used to the idea of doing a lot more in-class evaluating, with oral exams and live student presentations replacing homework and papers. How else can we ensure it's our students' work we're grading rather than a bot's? And what better incentive could we give them to seriously engage the material? While grading will become more time-intensive, perhaps we can enlist the help of AI to make it more manageable (an ironic twist!). I certainly wouldn't rush into this or trust AI to assign a grade without a great deal of customization and oversight (Mr. Garrison on South Park tried offloading his grading to ChatGPT and it did not end well). But perhaps with enough coordination and care, we can use the tool that caused the problem to help solve it—have AI transcribe and summarize students' oral exam answers, ask follow-up questions that we've pre-informed ("If they bring up theory X, ask them to apply it to issue Y"), record and provide content-specific links to video clips, as well as a preliminary grade and feedback for our review.

Maybe we'll innovate ourselves out of a job. Or maybe we'll just amplify our impact. At least until AI++ takes over.

# CHAPTER 11

# EARLY, AFTER, AND BEYOND ACADEMIA

According to the Association for Practical and Professional Ethics, Illinois Institute of Technology philosophy professor Bob Ladenson "first conducted an intramural Ethics Bowl tournament in 1993. Two years later he invited several nearby schools to take part, and in 1997 the APPE IEB was inaugurated as a national event with the organization of a competition involving 14 teams from colleges and universities throughout the United States."[57]

But while it may have been born in a college classroom, today Ethics Bowl is practiced in some form or fashion by elementary school students through retirees. As it should be. It's not like tough decisions begin in high school. And it's not like our perspectives cement in our 20s. I darn sure don't have everything figured out today, and suspect I never will.

The need for better, clearer, more informed choices takes root in our earliest years and persists through our

[57] APPE IEB History & Overview, updated April, 2020.

dying days. We remain constant students of the school of life.[58] This means that Ethics Bowl should begin early and run late. And I'm happy to report that's exactly what's happening.

## Starting Early Down Under

When it comes to sharing philosophy and ethics with the young, Ethics Olympiad has been ahead of most. Per usual, this is thanks to fearless leader Matthew Wills, who not only makes ethics and philosophy accessible and fun for college and high school students, but middle and elementary schoolers, too.

Since it's Matthew, you know he's going big. Middle School Ethics Olympiads in 2024 featured "over 1,800 *ethletes,* 250 coaches and 50 judge moderators,"[59] with teams not only from Australia, but New Zealand, India, Singapore, and Hong Kong. Matthew also does an exceptionally nice job organizing trainings for younger students. He makes a point to invite foreign speakers, and his patience managing guests in multiple time zones is an example for us all.

[58] This is beyond the scope of Ethics Bowl, but I personally recommend contemporary philosopher Alain De Botton's *School of Life* book series and YouTube videos. Though not every idea, of course. And my kids think he talks a little too much about sex.

[59] While Ethics Bowl usually separates the roles, Ethics Olympiad will often use a combined moderator-judge. I've done this, and it's not easy! But it is more efficient and requires fewer volunteers.

I may have botched my own Ethics Olympiad training Zoom presentation once, realizing while leaving my kids' soccer practice that I was scheduled to go live in mere moments. As I frantically joined via smartphone to disclose my mistake and buy some time, Matthew didn't let on even a hint of frustration. He simply stalled until I could get home, into a sportscoat and in front of a computer. I've gotten flustered as an online event organizer over far, far less. So extra kudos to Matthew for gracefully accommodating absentminded Yanks.

Thanks to him, I've had the pleasure of discussing ethics on several occasions with Australian elementary school students, and can confirm that they're just as eager as high schoolers and college students, and in many cases, more so. If you ever get the opportunity, one trick is to institute "the rule of three," which means if an especially eager student is talking a little too much, you can remind them that once they've spoken, they can only speak again once three others have had a turn (this works for overly eager college students, too).

You might worry kids this young would have trouble getting through a dense case set. But Matthew makes sure they're concise and often bases them on popular fiction with included video clips, sometimes simply of a narrator reading a children's book aloud, but other times of a key scene from a movie.

For example, the 2023 International Junior School Ethics Olympiad case package, for students aged 9 to 12, included "A Christmas Story – Responding to a Dare." The written details were only a few sentences long. But the case featured a picture of fourth graders Ralphie and Schwartz hyperlinked to a clip of classmate Flick succumbing to an irrefusable triple dog dare. The discussion questions:

1. Do you think that Flick really believes that his tongue won't stick to the post even though his friend has told him that his father saw it happen once?
2. What makes Flick do what his friends dare him to do?
3. If the other kids weren't there, do you think Flick would still have gone through with it?

Discussing poor Flick's freeze-stuck tongue might not feel as highbrow as the topics in most HSEB or IEB cases. But a) that's an awesome movie and b) being a little more lighthearted makes it more likely the kids will have a good time and return.

There's no reason leaders elsewhere couldn't craft similarly accessible and fun cases with accompanying multimedia for younger audiences. There's no reason the rest of the world couldn't successfully grow pre-high school Ethics Bowl, too. The only question is, who will have the vision and ambition to make it happen? Well, perhaps a Texan named Deric.

## Middle School Bowls Across America, Too

Several years ago, middle school teacher Deric Barber in Houston went in search of a new extracurricular for his students. He was looking for something that would engage their minds, expose them to issues and maybe build a little communication skill. As any thorough teacher in his shoes would do, he visited a nearby debate competition.

I'm sure not every debate is this way, but Deric happened to stumble into an especially bad one. Expecting lively but tasteful discussion, he was shocked by the belligerence of some teams. One in particular used the straw man tactic to bewilder their younger opponents, twisting and mercilessly attacking their view.

> The younger team wasn't ready… Anytime they tried to explain that the other team's (mis)interpretation was not what they had said, the aggressive team would grab the floor again… the aggressive team would talk over them and refuse to stop… Eventually a member of the younger team, having been bullied so aggressively and persistently, began to cry. What's worse is that the bullying team went on to win the tournament![60]

60 "'The Best?' – My Experience with Traditional Debate," August 31, 2022, ethicsbowl.org/2022/08/31/the-best-my-experience-with-traditional-debate/

Barber came away worried he wouldn't be able to find an activity worthy of his students' time. After all, when you're interested in contemporary issues and public speaking, debate has usually been the default option. Then he came across something new in the area called Ethics Bowl. Unsure of what the differences might be or whether this could be a viable alternative, he was invited to attend the Houston Area High School Ethics Bowl by organizer Adam Valenstein. Barber was absolutely thrilled by what he saw.

> Teams were not given a side to persuade others to—they created the best solution and let us/the other team know about their findings… to my amazement, the other team began saying, "Yes, we agree with your stance..." What? They were agreeing with the other team!? They went on to ask for more clarification on a certain way that the first team came to their conclusion and the floor was yielded to the first team to further explain their stance!... They were working together to find the best answer!

Barber was amazed that Ethics Bowl trusted teams to arrive at and defend their own views, that they were allowed to agree, and that truly civil discourse was not only expected, but happening before his eyes.

Supremely inspired, the following year Barber founded the first Middle School Ethics Bowl in the U.S., working with Valenstein to scrimmage against Houston high school teams, and then in 2018 brought together area middle schools for the first regional Middle School Bowl.

He's since gone on to work with PLATO, the Philosophy Learning and Teaching Organization co-founded by the Squire Family Foundation, to form a National Middle School Ethics Bowl executive committee responsible for spearheading middle school Bowl growth. In addition to Barber's regional Bowl in Texas, Kent Place in New Jersey hosts a regional competition for teams in New Jersey and New York, there's a regional in Philadelphia, another for teams in Rhode Island and Massachusetts, and local MSEBs in California, Oregon, and Washington.

It's exciting to see these take off for younger students here in the U.S., for the earlier we can instill Ethics Bowl's virtues and habits, the more impact it's likely to have. If you're a middle school educator and would like more info, I'd be happy to connect you directly with Barber. But you can also visit PLATO-philosophy.org and look for Philosophy Programs -> Programs for Young People -> Middle School Students -> Middle Schol Ethics Bowl. Thanks to Deric Barber, Roberta Israeloff, Jana M. Lone, and everyone involved for your awesome work.

## Ethics Slam!

For grownups itching to join the fun, A2Ethics in Ann Arbor has been a driving force behind "The Big Ethical Question Slam" or "Ethics Slam!" for short, a compressed Ethics Bowl derivative open to adults and often held in a bar.

Yes, a bar, which is consistent with A2Ethics's mission: to introduce ethical issues to the community in artful and inventive ways. From the website description:

> It's a "think-off" with oversized aspirations. That's the BIG part. It's also a congenial community get-together over drinks and eats to discuss the whats, hows and whys of doing the right thing. That's the ETHICAL QUESTION component. And it's an evening that makes an impact. That's where the SLAM comes in.

**A2ETHICS ETHICS SLAM 10TH ANNIVERSARY AT CONOR O'NEILL'S IRISH PUB** *COURTESY OF A2ETHICS*

Ethics Slam participants aren't expected to study a case set. But they are expected to don a jovial Cheers face (remember the characters in the black-and-white photos during the show's intro song? "Sometimes you wanna go, where everybody knows your naaa-ame…") and partake in a spirited discussion. And with team names like "The Feminosophers," "Kant Touch This," and "We Nietzshe To

Buy Us A Round," the mood is definitely merry and light.

Weber State University in Utah has also been a strong proponent of Ethics Slam, though their Slams are more likely to be held in a coffeeshop. Managed by philosophy professor and longtime Ethics Bowl leader Richard Greene, timely Utah Slam topics have included "Pandemic Ethics" in 2020, "The Ethics of Anti-DEI Legislation" in 2024, and both "Ethics and Chatbots" and "The Ethics of Civil Disobedience" in 2025.

Ethics Slams have been held in some form or fashion at James Madison University in Virginia, Baylor University in Texas, the University of Manitoba in Canada, and the University of Queensland in Australia. The University of North Florida even hosts *Philosophy* Slams, which sometimes cover ethical questions, but also fun and disturbing philosophical questions such as, "Are we living in a simulation?" For the record, we are not living in a simulation. Stop being so weird, epistemologists.

If you're inspired to join Ethics Bowl, but the idea of coaching, judging, or even simply moderating doesn't seem the best fit, look into Ethics Slam. If you're nowhere near the places already hosting Slams, no sweat. Jeanine DeLay with A2Ethics or Richard Greene with Weber State are sure to be willing to share materials. And if you're the host, you can decide whether your own Slam is lubricated with alcohol, caffeine, or something else. Possibly protein smoothies in Venice, CA, hot chocolate in Hershey, PA, or Cheerwine soda anywhere in the South (*not* moonshine—trust me).

## Yes, Even in Retirement Communities

When I think of retirement, two things come to mind: bingo and Florida. Which is probably Jerry Seinfeld's fault. While his fictional sitcom parents, Morty and Helen, may have never participated in an Ethics Bowl, they could have were they near Gainesville and Santa Fe College.

Thanks in part to a grant from the National Endowment for the Humanities, the Santa Fe IEB team began discussing Ethics Bowl cases with residents of Oak Hammock retirement community in 2020. In their initial presentation, topics included the climate impact of taking long flights (which retirees are known for), how to respectfully disagree with your elders (which retirees with uppity children may want to discuss), and whether blind and low vision persons should own guns (a topic extra-relevant for folks with neighbors with aging eyes).

Now part of Santa Fe College's Institute of Learning in Retirement, their IEB team's ongoing partnership with Oak Hammock is pitched as an opportunity for productive cross-generational interaction.

> These popular and engaging discussions bring to light the benefits and challenges of intergenerational dialogue. Participants agree - it's time well spent![61]

[61] "Ethics Initiatives at SF," sfcollege.edu/academics/las/hcl/applied-ethics-and-humanities/ethics-initiatives-at-sf.html

However, this apparently wasn't the first time an Ethics Bowl discussion took place in a retirement community. Way back in 2013, Buffalo State University's IEB team in New York (less than thirty minutes from beautiful Niagara Falls, but more than a six-hour drive from Jerry, Elaine, Kramer, and George in Manhattan) was already visiting seniors at the Canterbury Woods Life Care Community in Williamsville.

This was in part a generous act of public philosophy outreach. But it was also an ingenious way to prepare for their IEB regional. Journalist Laurie Kaiser pointed out how many Canterbury Woods residents were not only Buffalo State alum, but "former doctors, business professionals, and teachers."[62] Philosophy professor and IEB coach Julian Cole noted how discussing cases with retirees exposed the team to ideas they might have otherwise never considered.

> I think the students get a lot of different perspectives from the residents here... It is particularly helpful that the conversation is intergenerational as this brings students into contact with perspectives that, in some cases, they encounter infrequently.

[62] "Ethics Bowl Team Gains Insight from Older Generation," February 26, 2013, newsarchive.buffalostate.edu/news/ethics-bowl-team-gains-insight-older-generation

Given how different Boomers, Xers, Millennials, and Gen Zers are purported to be, and how we tend to self-segregate and blame one another for everything, it's great that Ethics Bowl is not only facilitating cross-generational conversations, but cross-generational wisdom sharing, and cross-generational kinship. For retirees, perhaps they can see where they've been in the younger folks. For the IEB teams, perhaps they can imagine where they'll one day be.

Like few other activities, Ethics Bowl reveals and affirms our common experience as moral creatures. And it's heartening to learn that we're finding a receptive audience in our seniors, and that they're eagerly engaging with our ethics-minded youth. But beyond retirement communities, there's one setting where our shared humanity is in even more need of affirmation and reinforcement.

# CHAPTER 12

# BOWLS BEHIND BARS?

One place you might not expect to find Ethics Bowls is in prisons. Then again, there was once a somewhat famous philosopher who did some of his best work while behind bars. We know this because conversations with friends who came to visit were later published. One friend tried to convince him to escape, even offering to help, which led to a discussion on the nature of justice and citizens' duties.

On the final day, talk turned to logical arguments concerning the immortality of the soul. The imprisoned philosopher concluded that our soul most likely does survive bodily death, which might have made his ultimate sentence a little easier to bear. Anyway, you may have heard of him—Socrates?

While Socrates's dialogues with Crito, Phaedo, Simmias, and others may not have constituted an Ethics Bowl, Ethics Bowls have been held in prisons in at least five U.S. states. And as you might imagine, they're an opportunity to not only enhance moral reasoning, but to humanize, teach empathy and compassion for all involved.

## San Quentin Pioneers

In the first known case, University of California Santa Cruz philosophy professor, IEB coach, and Northern California HSEB organizer, Kyle Robertson, coached a group of students at San Quentin State Prison (later renamed San Quentin Rehabilitation Center) in late 2017, then brought his IEB team to hold a friendly match in early 2018. Writing for UC Santa Cruz, Scott Rappaport covered the event, as well as the background leading up to it.

> Twice a month from last September to February, UC Santa Cruz philosophy lecturer Kyle Robertson woke up early, dropped his kids off at school, drove north for one hour and fifty minutes, crossed the Richmond Bridge, and went to San Quentin.
>
> He would park in the prison lot, walk past a gift shop selling art created by death row inmates, and enter the main gate, where he would sign in at the first of three consecutive checkpoints. Finally entering the prison yard, he would walk past prisoners playing on the basketball courts and others engaged in games of chess, to get to the education center of the prison.
>
> Robertson was there to teach a course in Ethics Bowl—a non-confrontational alternative to the traditional competitive form of debate—in collaboration with the Prison University Project (PUP). At the same time, he was also teaching an

> undergraduate course and coaching a team in Ethics Bowl at UC Santa Cruz. He soon suggested and arranged a very unusual debate between seven philosophy students from UC Santa Cruz and a team of prison inmates from San Quentin. It took place in the prison chapel—in front of an audience of nearly 100 inmates.[63]

UC Santa Cruz IEB team member Pedro Enriquez was there that day. He was a junior at the time and recalled his initial unease.

> I thought it was going to be a lot more like the movies where they're locked down, and you know, they're going to be hollering or whatever. So when we walked in after we passed the security and they were just walking around, I was like, "Wait, is anybody gonna do anything? Like, where are all the cops? What if they do something?"[64]

Enriquez and his teammates quickly realized they were safe. And when apart from an interruption for a mandatory headcount, the rounds progressed per usual. The San Quentin team took the trophy, the UC Santa Cruz IEB team returned the next year, and word soon spread.

63 "How to Find Truth in Today's Partisan World" by Scott Rappaport for UC Santa Cruz's Center for Public Philosophy, reports.news.ucsc.edu/ethics-bowl
64 Ibid.

## Contagious Compassion

Among the judges that day was none other than Ethics Bowl creator Bob Ladenson who had moved to California to be closer to his grandkids after retiring from the Illinois Institute of Technology. At his side was the IEB director at the time, professor Richard Greene from Weber State University in Utah. Greene spoke with many of the imprisoned students and was so impressed by their seriousness and dedication that he worked with Rachel Robison-Greene of Utah State University to found a similar program in Utah. By the spring of 2020, they had an Ethics Bowl class in both the men's and women's state prisons.

COVID derailed their efforts temporarily. But they restarted in 2023, and after an eight-week class, two Utah IEB teams, one from Weber State and another from Utah State, visited for a friendly at the women's facility. Greene had nothing but good things to say about the event, as well as his experience working with the students.

> It was a glorious event. The incarcerated students' hard work paid off with a convincing win in one match and a close loss in the other. They were extremely proud of themselves and in some cases the incarcerated students reported surprising themselves... I find working with the incarcerated students to be extremely rewarding. They exhibit much gratitude and I always leave the classroom

> feeling empowered and feeling like I've been able to make some difference in some of their lives.

Utah Valley University philosophy professor and founder of the Utah High School Ethics Bowl Karen Mizell was a judge that day. Similar to Greene's experience at San Quentin, Mizell left determined to recruit colleagues to hold a Bowl at the men's facility as well. They got busy coaching, sharing how Ethics Bowl works, teaching case analysis strategies and ethical theories. Students couldn't access the internet, and materials carried in had to be reviewed for approval. Nevertheless, Mizell's faith that the students would be worth the extra effort was confirmed.

> The group was thoughtful, serious, and collaborative. By the end of the semester, they were ready for a formal match against our nationally ranked UVU team. The competition was sharp, respectful, and well-argued.

One of the cases was on a conflict between a deceased donor's trust and the way a foundation their estate funded was handling a work of art. Mizell shared how a student had come across a news story of a similar situation and taken the time to share it with her through a colleague working at the prison along with a handwritten note.

> It came from a student in the class who had stood out as a steady, insightful presence throughout the

course. In his note, he thanked us for the experience on behalf of his fellow classmates and enclosed a New York Times newspaper clipping about the Museum Langmatt in Switzerland, which had announced plans to auction several Cezanne paintings to manage their financial challenges. The student made the connection to the Barnes Foundation case we had studied together during the semester, where Albert C. Barnes' clear instructions were overridden…

Given the lack of internet access, the fact that this student came across a comparable situation and thought to pass it along was deeply affirming, and a reminder of the kind of lasting engagement the activity cultivates among participants. That moment reflected something we saw often during the semester: careful attention to case details, a willingness to wrestle with moral complexity, and a strong sense of intellectual curiosity. The students took their preparation seriously, supported one another, and built an atmosphere of real respect and inquiry. Ethics Bowl turned out to be a useful structure for that kind of work. It gave them a shared language, a community space to reason together, and a framework they could carry forward. And sometimes, it circled back in unexpected ways.

Kyle Robertson's work at San Quentin had inspired judge Richard Greene to bring Ethics Bowl to prisons in Utah, whose work inspired judge Karen Mizell to expand them further. But word was spreading elsewhere.

In 2019, Paul Tubig, who was a grad student at the University of Washington, brought Ethics Bowl to the Washington Corrections Center for Women (WCCW). Tubig had coached a high school Ethics Bowl team and was already teaching Intro to Philosophy at WCCW. So when one of his students expressed interest in a debate-like competition, he recalled hearing about Roberton's work at San Quentin and decided to give it a go. The team studied individually during the week, then met with coach Tubig to train for a few hours Saturday evenings.

After several months of preparation, they were ready to compete against an IEB team from the University of Puget Sound. Topics included whether to de-extinct lost species, whether terminally ill children should be allowed to choose euthanasia, and whether rich countries owe a climate debt to poorer countries.[65] Puget Sound's IEB team ultimately won. But Tubig's WCCW students had thoroughly prepared and kept the match extremely close—as Matthew Wills in Australia might say, falling short only "by a cat's whisker."

65 "Doctoral Candidate Paul Tubig Organized the First Ever Intercollegiate Ethics Bowl at The Washington Corrections Center for Women" by Kate Godyn for the University of Washington Philosophy Department's website, May 13, 2019.

THE WASHINGTON CORRECTIONS CENTER FOR WOMEN TEAM SHAKING HANDS WITH THE UNIVERSITY OF PUGENT SOUND'S IEB TEAM AFTER THEIR FRIENDLY MATCH *COURTESY OF PAUL TUBIG*

What made the WCCW team even more impressive was that they went on to compete in the 2019 Northwest Regional Intercollegiate Ethics Bowl. Though they could only join via Zoom, they confirmed that when given the chance, incarcerated students can contribute meaningfully to democratic dialogue, even among undergraduates from leading universities. A philosophy professor at Georgia Southern University today, Tubig reflected on his initial motivations of making philosophy accessible, as well as the value of Ethics Bowls in prisons.

> For me, the underlying value of bringing the Ethics Bowl to incarcerated students was to give them access to a meaningful, intellectually stimulating, and dignity-affirming activity. Prison is an environment that disciplines the behaviors of its captives in punitive ways, limiting their physical

> freedom and freedom of expression. Giving incarcerated students the opportunity to participate in an intellectually stimulating and mentally emancipatory activity like Ethics Bowl has the potential to disrupt the dull monotony, restlessness, and degradation of prison life by having them exercise their freedom of the mind and legitimate their voices as worthy of consideration and integration in the broader community of philosophical and ethical inquiry. I mainly did Ethics Bowls for my students, but I also hoped their participation helped destigmatize incarcerated students.

## Eastbound and Down

From California to Utah to Washington state, there are at least two Ethics Bowl in prisons programs on the East Coast. First, thanks to Tufts University senior distinguished philosophy lecturer Susan Russinoff, who also organizes the New England High School Ethics Bowl and coaches Tufts's IEB team, the Tufts University Prison Initiative of Tisch College (TUPIT) hosted a Bowl at the Massachusetts Correctional Institute in Concord in 2019. Returning for a second Bowl in 2022, Russinoff worked with her IEB students to recruit and coach two TUPIT teams.

On Bowl day, the Tufts IEB students judged, while TUPIT students who had competed in 2019 served as team leaders and moderators. Their engagement in Bowl coordination and sustainment may be a first.

Param Upadhyay was a judge that day, and similar to judges out West, was struck by how focused and present the TUPIT students were, and how mindfully they listened and responded to one another. But the fact that TUPIT students were not only competing, but assisting in the event's organization, took their involvement to another level. Sometimes roles reversed and they even coached the judges. One of the cases was on "doxing," which is when a person's personal information is exposed online without their consent. While Upadhyay was trying to think of a good question to ask during the judge Q&A, one of the TUPIT moderators gave him some friendly advice. As reported by Taylor McNeil for Tufts Now:

> One of the moderators, from the 2019 incarcerated student group, leaned over to him and said in reference to the doxing question, "Ask about snitching." He did, and all the students understood the nuanced connection between doxing on the outside and snitching on the inside. "Everyone just started laughing, and people said, 'Oh my God, he got us,'" Upadhyay said.[66]

Finally, Salisbury University in Maryland has been hosting an Ethics Bowl at Eastern Correctional Institution

[66] "Learning Ethics in Prison" by Taylor McNeil for Tufts Now, November 14, 2022.

since 2021, and their participants are so good, they've expanded from competing against Salisbury's IEB team to case writing. And not just any old cases. If you review the first page of the 2024 IEB regional case set, you'll find the note:

> Three of the following cases have been developed through the Ethics Bowl program at the Eastern Correctional Institution Libraries, in partnership with Salisbury University's Department of Philosophy.

To develop a program of this caliber, Salisbury's philosophy department recruits, trains, and sends teams of three undergrads into ECI to lead discussions with groups of around ten incarcerated students for three to six weeks. Goals include covering "thinkers such as Socrates and Sartre, and themes such as love, freedom, and justice, as well as developing skills together in articulating the nature of right and wrong actions and ethical decision making."

The online application ensures volunteers understand the commitment required, as well as the risks. And they're asked to check their egos at the front gate. Visiting students are encouraged to conduct themselves not as teachers, "but rather act as guides with tolerant, and open-minded attitudes, a willingness to learn from their group members including inmates, and an aspiration to see truth." Gaining approval to participate isn't easy. But for those who make the cut, a transformative experience awaits, confirmed by Salisbury student and program participant Jon Wirth.

> [It is in] brief moments, when I am not only a twenty-some-year-old college student talking with a twenty-some-year-old inmate about Socrates, Gandhi, Shakespeare, Poe, King or Dostoevsky, when I am not… teaching, but learning the truth, that this program affirms its value. The ECI program [allowed me] the opportunity to discuss… subjects such as freedom, bondage, violence, and non-violence… with individuals for whom they are imminent situations, [and] has been one of the most rewarding experiences of my life.[67]

Today, the original San Quentin Bowl continues to thrive thanks to partnership between UC Santa Cruz and Mount Tamalpais College, whose purpose "is to provide an intellectually rigorous, inclusive Associate of Arts degree program and College Preparatory Program, free of charge, to people at San Quentin Rehabilitation Center."[68] Granted accreditation as an independent 2-year liberal arts college in 2022, Mount Tam's values include critical thinking,

[67] Fulton School of Liberal Arts, Philosophy Department, Eastern Correctional Institution Program: salisbury.edu/academic-offices/liberal-arts/philosophy/eci-program.aspx
[68] mttamcollege.edu/about/mission-vision

respectful dialog, human dignity, and civil discourse. So it's no surprise that they've embraced Ethics Bowl as a natural extension of their mission.

And while it might have initially been surprising to imagine Ethics Bowls in prisons, the work of Robertson, Greene, Mizell, Tubig, Rusinoff, and others proves that there's nothing unnatural about the pairing. After all, one of the greatest philosophers of all time did some of his best work behind bars. And if Ethics Bowl is about anything, it's about compassion and human dignity.

THE MOUNT TAMALPAIS COLLEGE ETHICS BOWL TEAM AT SAN QUENTIN WITH JUDGES AND COACHES - PROGRAM FOUNDER KYLE ROBERTSON BACK ROW, FIRST ON LEFT *COURTESY OF MOUNT TAMALPAIS COLLEGE*

# CHAPTER 13
# MAKE IT MANDATORY?

If you're as excited about Ethics Bowl as I hope you are, we have an important question to consider. And that question is whether to leave it voluntary and comparatively rare or to push to make it mandatory.

Some might argue that while Ethics Bowls are cool, they're unnecessary. Highbrow moral discussion occurs naturally. Why spend the time and effort organizing something that happens on its own?

Because for one, it doesn't happen enough. And for another, while I try to avoid the "c" word, competition drives excellence.

Martial artists know this well. A few Bruce Lee types would hone their craft for the pure pleasure of physical mastery. Ah, but knowing you'll face a resistant opponent, in front of a crowd and referee—that's what pushes boxers, judokas, and karatekas to sweat, drill, and ultimately elevate their game to real-world applicable levels. My two youngest kids and I competed in our first jiu jitsu tournament this summer, and knowing that those rolls would be less than friendly pushed all three of us to train extra hard. We won some and lost some. But agreeing to compete and seeing that date on the calendar accelerated our growth far faster than casual sparring.

The same could be said for air guitarists, cheese rollers, or spelling bee contestants. How many would memorize *onomatopoeia* without the anticipation of a legit, public test? Without competition, we have less incentive to improve. And yes, air guitar and cheese rolling contests are real. And awesome.

A similar problem persists when our views on moral and social issues go untested. When strangers politely agree with us and friends cheer our confirmation of their biases, we assume we must have it all figured out. Our insulated thought bubble allows weak ideas to pass as unassailable, we suffer false confidence, and support things we otherwise wouldn't as a result.

Of course, most of us think this only applies to the other guys. *Our* views really are high quality. *Our* tribe really has thought things through. One reason most of us believe this is because our favored champions tend to pit our preferred views against powder puff critiques.

## Ethics Bowl as Idea Lab

In his 2023 stick figure-illustrated book, *What's Our Problem? A Self-Help Book for Societies,* eclectic blogger Tim Urban explains this common practice of tribes inflating their superiority by defending their views against weak objections, similar to how boxing promoters will pad the record of a mediocre fighter by only accepting matches against weak opponents. Urban gives examples of presidents from both sides of American politics shooting down distortions of Republicans' or Democrats' objections to their policies, then undeservedly gloating.

This is of course a form of the classic "straw man" logical fallacy. Rather than confronting a reasonable objection a thoughtful human might offer in good faith, you just pretend anyone who disagrees with you must believe obvious foolishness, then celebrate your brilliance, reassured that you're right, they're wrong, na-na-na-boo-boo.

Manipulative reasoning like this is unfortunately common, and apparently too effective to resist. Urban offers it as an example of "low-rung" caveman-like thinking on a ladder of better or worse reasoning. High-minded scientist-like thinking occupies the top rung, with lawyer and sports fan thinking in between, all to a greater or lesser extent interested in "winning" versus the truth. Urban points out that while both sides of traditional American politics are blessed by groups of high-rung scientist-types—he calls the collective positive brainpower of these groups "genies"—both sides are also plagued by factions of low-rung caveman-types—he calls their combined destructive influence "golems."

Depending on your sympathies and what news sources you frequent, you may be more aware of the Red golem or Blue golem, or the Red genie or Blue genie. But Urban's correct that both sides have them, and while it's encouraging that principled, moral people can be found in both camps (I promise—they can!), it's bad news that both camps' golems are becoming increasingly powerful, thanks largely to hyperpartisan traditional media and Wild West extremifying muck-and-lies social media. But what if there were a solution…

We're all familiar with the term echo chamber: the constraining ideological ecosystem we get trapped in when platforms attempting to maximize our attention (which they then sell) expose us to content we're most likely to view, click, and share, which unfortunately is often the content that makes us afraid or angry. We tune in our favorite pundits so we can feel correct, but also to see what awfulness the other side is up to.

Obviously, this is a toxic environment. There ain't much progress happening when everyone's trapped in doom loop echo chamber rage spirals. We're made more suspicious, more fearful, more angry, which only empowers opportunists eager to exploit our vulnerable condition. The result: our collective ability to justly self-govern is destroyed. Democratic peoples *need* forums where high-rung thinking can flourish without low-rung distractions. And Urban calls this opposite of an echo chamber an Idea Lab.

> An Idea Lab is an environment of collaborative high-rung thinking. People in an Idea Lab see one another as experimenters and their ideas as experiments. Idea

Labs value independent thinking and viewpoint diversity. This combination leads to the richest and most interesting conversations and maximizes the scope of group discussions.

Idea Labs place a high regard on humility, and saying "I don't know" usually wins trust and respect… Idea Labs also love arguments. Ideas in an Idea Lab are treated like hypotheses, which means people are always looking for opportunities to test what they've been thinking about. Idea Labs are the perfect boxing ring for that testing...

Perhaps most importantly, an Idea Lab helps its members stay high up on the Ladder. No one thinks like pure top-rung Scientists all the time. More often, after a brief stint on the top rung during an especially lucid and humble period, we start to like the new epiphanies we gleaned up there a little too much, and we quickly drop down to the Sports Fan rung. And that's okay. It might even be optimal to be a little over-confident in our intellectual lives. Rooting for our ideas—a new philosophy, a new lifestyle choice, a new business strategy—allows us to really give them a try, somewhat liberated from the constant "but are we really sure about this?" nag from the Higher Mind...

> This is why Idea Lab culture is so important. It's a support network for flawed thinkers to help each other stay up on the high rungs.
>
> The social pressure helps. If high-rung thinking is what all the cool kids are doing, you're more likely to think that way.
>
> And the intellectual pressure helps. In an Idea Lab—where people don't hesitate to tell you when you're wrong or biased or hypocritical or gullible —humility and self-awareness are inflicted upon you. Whenever you get a little too overconfident, Idea Lab culture pulls you back to an honest level of conviction.
>
> All these forces combine to make an Idea Lab a big magnet on top of the Ladder that pulls upward on the psyches of people immersed in it.[69]

Man, this Tim Urban guy is really onto something. If only there were an Idea Lab contest or game we could implement in our school systems and start demanding our so-called leaders model it and *OMG has anyone told this beautiful man about Ethics Bowl?!*

[69] Kindle edition, page 66.

## The "Competition" Complaint

Idea Labs could arise organically. But do they? Not from what I've seen. Not on Twitter, not on television, not in the halls of Congress.[70] All of these *could* be Idea Labs. But they almost never are.

However, Ethics Bowls are simple, inexpensive, established Idea Labs—near perfect forums for thinking through tough moral and political questions in a civil, highbrow fashion. I haven't emphasized this enough, but I *learn* at Ethics Bowls. Teams typically aren't parroting partisan propaganda. They're innovating, uncovering new insights, working together to find principled solutions.

Accordingly, I think more energy needs to be devoted to sharing how Ethics Bowlers are arguing so the rest of us can take notice. My local PBS station broadcasts scholars bowls, which are worthwhile, but concern random trivia. ESPN has been known to televise spelling bees. Spelling bees! How about the semifinals and championship round of the next IEB? Narrated highlights would do. So long as the upshots are digestible and sharable, let's do more to spread whatever moral breakthroughs these Idea Lab

[70] I share my experience discussing the deliberative process with a former congressperson in the opening chapter of *Abortion Ethics in a Nutshell: A Pro-Both Tour of the Moral Arguments*. Spoiler: if earnest discussions over difficult issues are going to happen, they're going to have to happen among us. Because most elected officials believe their job is to enforce a settled worldview, not cooperatively seek truth.

scientists are discovering.[71]

All that said, I know the fact that Ethics Bowl is a competition seems counterintuitive. We're supposed to be very different from a typical debate. The "contest" part feels out of place. So, any pro-cooperation instincts you might have aren't without merit, and you're in very good company. Organizer and Texas Regional High School Ethics Bowl-winning coach Adam Valenstein shared how he remembers Ethics Bowlers wishing aloud that we could find ways to de-emphasize winners vs. losers.

> I was in Chapel Hill for the NHSEB, and we were riding in the hotel shuttle to the competition with another team. We struck up a friendly conversation, and both teams were sharing their appreciation for the Bowl. Towards the end, a young woman from the other team said something along the lines of: "I just love the conversations. There really shouldn't be a winner." Everyone in the van nodded in agreement and a thoughtful silence filled the cabin. She was right.

While I think the benefits of competing outweigh the drawbacks, it is indeed a shame that judges have to choose a

[71] If you'd like to report on reasons shared and arguments made at Ethics Bowls for EthicsBowl.org, please contact me. Just keep in mind that accessibility and conciseness are key. It's a blog, not an academic journal. But if you're down with pithy prose, reach out.

winner. Announcing winners is one of my least favorite parts of Ethics Bowl, second only to filling out score sheets. However, scoring pushes teams to do the work.[72] And this is why it's appropriate to frame it as a competition, and why we can't simply hope Ethics Bowl-like benefits would come about on their own.

With an Ethics Bowl on the calendar, teams know they'll face analysis from a tactful but challenging team. They know kind but unconstrained judges will ask tough questions and score responses according to their rational quality. Michigan HSEB organizer Jeanine DeLay of A2Ethics agrees that the format just works.

> Ethics Bowl builds into its structure an unusual form of teamwork, in which teammates themselves disagree with each other and try to work out how they can contend with their own disagreements *before* they go to the Bowl table and present their ideas and insights to other teams and judges.

Dave Weber, organizer of the Oregon HSEB, argues the same—that while the culminating celebration of an Ethics Bowl competition may be necessary (and awesome), it's the work completed beforehand driving the real growth.

[72] For opportunities to do philosophy and ethics noncompetitively, check out PLATO's various offerings at Plato-philosophy.org.

> As I announce every year on the day of the competition—Aristotle says that pleasure completes the activity; and this competition completes the activity of the past few months. But it's the past few months that constitute that important activity that is the Ethics Bowl.

## So Why Not Make It Mandatory?

If Ethics Bowl is a simple, established, and much-needed Idea Lab, if all this good comes from having a competition on the calendar, and if the benefits are as impressive as we believe, the question becomes whether we should move from voluntary to required participation. No one's suggesting forcing Ethics Slam onto the daily activities schedule at the retirement home. But Ethics Bowl could be added to the standard school year. But would this be a good idea?

Arguing in the affirmative is Justin McBrayer, the Fort Lewis College philosophy professor we met in chapter 9. Recall how he argued in favor of providing Ethics Bowlers clearer guidance on handling empirical disagreements, in part because hot issues are becoming increasingly distorted by bad-faith factual framing. As an expert on misinformation and social divisions, McBrayer understands the dangers we're facing better than most, and has concluded that public discourse is so broken that Ethics Bowl or some similarly civilizing variant should be compulsory.

> Given the renewed interest in civil education (given the polarized and violent political times we find ourselves in), every school in a functioning democracy should mandate participation in Ethics Bowl or similar exercises.

I agree that we're living through unusually polarized times. But making Ethics Bowl mandatory could be a drastic step. In most places, not even civics is required anymore. And sometimes forcing a good thing turns it bad.

While HSEB coach Michael Andersen in Washington shares McBrayer's enthusiasm for Ethics Bowl's transformative power, he worries forcing participation could spoil the spirit.

> I only wish that this activity could formally become a part of the humanities instruction in public and private schools across the country. It's an open question, however, whether Ethics Bowl, as a compulsory element of the curriculum, would enhance the overall quality of the experience for students. Perhaps its magic comes from its extracurricular and voluntary nature?

Would obligatory Ethics Bowl kill the fun the way mandatory gym class ruins the glorious sport of dodgeball? I think recruiting participants with an arm twist rather than a smile would indeed degrade the atmosphere. Maybe the benefits would be worth it. But we need to appreciate how shoving all students outside of their comfort zones rather than welcoming a willing few would cause increased drama and stress.

So far, Ethics Bowl has tended to appeal most to a minority of students with a certain disposition. They're known for openness, inquisitiveness and, most importantly, bravery. Ethics conversations may not be as scary as taking a dodgeball to the face. But dodgeballs can be ducked. When they land, the sting is fleeting.

Our moral and political views, on the other hand, are entwined with our identities—some believe even our immortal souls. Sharing them, or simply sharing ambivalence or doubt about them, can leave us labeled an "other," a "heretic," one of "them." Few of us enjoy being an outcast, and so there have been times I've been intimidated into silence, keeping quiet, self-censoring out of fear of being branded. Many conscripted Ethics Bowl participants would feel similar pressure to conform, causing anxiety and resentment.

There's also the fear of having cherished convictions shaken, especially when your commitment to them feels like a commitment to the groups and ideologies that give you meaning and esteem. I remember chaffing at my first ethics professor, at even the suggestion that a know-it-all academic might have some insight into morality I hadn't already learned from family or church. On the surface, I had everything figured out and little need for additional instruction. But secretly, I was terrified she would reveal a weakness I wouldn't be able to explain—a weakness that might cause me to reevaluate my views and put me at odds with family, fellow servicemembers (I was in the Air National Guard at the time) or my faith.

Insecurity like this partially explains the "Backfire Effect," a cognitive bias where we're tempted to strengthen rather than weaken cherished beliefs when they're challenged with disconfirming evidence. Imagine a group of grudging teenagers mutually sabotaging what could have been a fruitful Ethics Bowl discussion, all because they were forced to be there and are understandably afraid they'll come to a realization that could break their parents' hearts. Coaches have a hard enough time building trust with Bowlers who join voluntarily.

Then there's pride. For all my preaching about disentangling our egos from our views and following reason wherever it leads, there have been times that I've been reluctant to change my mind simply because it would require conceding to a rival. When you've been hurt, it's really, really hard to admit those who hurt you might have been correct. And I'm a reasonably mature and secure grown man. How could we expect better from kids?

For these understandable reasons and others, many students prefer to avoid engagement and to fade into the background. They know how the tentative views we share today can follow us long after we've rethought matters, and would be reluctant to openly discuss many of the topics

Ethics Bowl covers. Especially in the current political climate, remaining neutral rather than risking a stigmatizing label seems prudent. Even when we're around people who seem reasonable enough, what if word got back to the militant hooligans? And even absent hooligans, moral discussions can feel intrusive, threatening our relationships and sense of self-worth.

Requiring students to be subjected to that sort of vulnerability could cause a backlash the Ethics Bowl movement could do without. Yet, if we're drinking our own Kool-Aid, how can we not push it as heavy-handedly as we can get away with?

## One Solution

I share McBrayer's sense of need, yet Andersen's hesitance. Would spiteful draftees poison the morale of an otherwise all-volunteer Ethics Bowl army? They would. Could making it mandatory cause resentment, disruptions, and revolt? Yes. But is there desperate need for all the benefits Ethics Bowl has to offer, a need that will only be partially satisfied if participation is isolated to students already inclined to reason respectfully and collaboratively? For sure.

One solution could be to require it at select ages. This would make the awkwardness and dread manageable, yet ensure everyone gets a feel. It would recruit lifelong advocates who otherwise might've never known Ethics

Bowl existed. And it would serve as an intervention for the would-be boisterous blowhards who need it most.

Just imagine how our current political climate would be different if everyone had experienced Ethics Bowl as a high school junior or senior.

Temporary challenges experienced together are easier to accept, making a universal but contained Ethics Bowl requirement more tolerable for students and parents alike. That particular semester in that particular grade in that particular class could become an accepted rite of passage, similar to the shared learning for college freshmen at some universities, where everyone reads and discusses the same book regardless of major.

Of course, no school can send hundreds of students to compete in a traditional Ethics Bowl. Most organizers limit the number of teams a school can send to three, and with three-to-seven students per team, twenty-one would be the typical max.

Solution: intra-school or simply intra-class Bowls with flexible team sizes. "Ethics Bowl for the Classroom" is a simple guide available for free on the Resources page at EthicsBowl.org, It's not rocket science. You divide the class into teams, give them time to study cases, and run a Bowl per usual, recruiting the custodian to help judge if you're shorthanded. You can hold out for bigger regional Bowls if you like. But if you're interested in being part of the solution sooner rather than later, a free guide and simple moderator script await.

If you're a school principal sold on the model, consider inviting your debate coach to try it. But also talk to your History, Government, Social Studies, Civics, and even English faculty, see if any are willing to run a pilot, perhaps working it into the last fifteen minutes on Fridays, full class periods once per month, or for a devoted week once annual tests are complete. There are natural lulls in the academic calendar. Why not put them to good use? Especially in light of Michael Prinzing and Michael Vazquez's recent study from chapter 6, "Studying Philosophy Does Make People Better Thinkers," your reasons can be to both promote civility and improve test scores—nothing wrong with converging motivations.

If you're a school superintendent, here's your ammunition. If you're a principal, here's your plan. If you're a professor, teacher, or debate coach, let's go! Don't wait for someone to voluntell you. And don't worry that making Ethics Bowl mandatory will ruin it. Create and expand fully voluntary options for those who love it. But see what you can do to ensure everyone gets a taste.

# CHAPTER 14

# JOIN US!

Would supplanting debate with Ethics Bowl deliver a utopia? Of course not. People would continue to quarrel. Factions would still divide. Deception and treachery would live on, both in our personal and public lives.

However, expanding Ethics Bowl would make fruitful, dignified discussion more commonplace. It would foster humility and principled compromise. It's not unreasonable to expect that more Ethics Bowl would mean more justice, for justice is in part revealed and produced when issues are settled together, in a spirit of shared discovery rather than combat.

**2024 IEB NATIONALS OPENING CEREMONY** *COURTESY OF APPE IEB®*

Ethics Bowl could even increase charitable giving and volunteer work, decrease addiction and crime. But no need to overpromise. It's taken for granted that it's a strategic, slow growth solution, not a quick fix.

But since we're fresh out of quick fixes, perhaps phasing out a known corruptor and phasing in a promising rejuvenator is worth the minimal effort. And I say minimal effort because the framework is there. Convince a critical mass in the debate community to join us and bam—Ethics Bowl to the rescue!

## Predictable Resistance

You can tell I'm convinced. But some will remain skeptical, and many will be downright hostile. When your tribe possesses the complete, unassailable truth, what good could come of discussion?

But we know bluster is often a mask. 20th century American thinker and rabbi Joshua Liebman colorfully reminds us how humility is an undeniable virtue, how dealing with the close-minded is a fact of life, and how our own moral growth is a never-ending project.

> Dense, unenlightened people are notoriously confident that they have the monopoly on truth; if you need proof, feel the weight of their knuckles. But anyone with the faintest glimmerings of imagination knows that truth is broader than any individual conception of it, stronger than any fist. Recall, too, how many earnestly held opinions and emotions we

> have outgrown with the passage of years. Given a little luck, plus a lively sense of the world about us, we shall probably outgrow many more. [19th century French philosopher Ernest] Renan's remark that our opinions become fixed at the point where we stop thinking should be sufficient warning against premature hardening of our intellectual arteries, or too stubborn insistence that we are infallibly and invariably right.[73]

I've been dense and unenlightened on many things. On some, I probably still am. But just as courage begets courage, vulnerability begets vulnerability. My own intellectual arteries may not flow as freely as they once did. But witnessing the variety of thought at an Ethics Bowl, and participants' willingness to share and adopt novel lines of reasoning, helps dissolve the plaque.

## But Does It Even Work?

Others will dismiss Ethics Bowl's benefits as superficial, challenging ethical discussion's ability to translate into ethical action. We can direct this camp to George Sherman.

I foreshadowed the great St. George of St. Petersburg College, Florida in previous chapters. Organizer, judge, ambassador, and fan, the tall philosophy professor in jeans

73 *Peace of Mind: Insights on Human Nature That Can Change Your Life*. Carol Publishing Group, 1946, page 76.

and a sports coat has been a fixture in the Ethics Bowl community for as long as I can remember. He's the guy who so eloquently argued that Ethics Bowl develops participants' "BS detectors," enabling them to identify BS—"even their own." And when it comes to passion and commitment, his ranks up there with Ethics Bowl creator Bob Ladenson's.

George has been busy serving in almost every role possible, on both the collegiate and high school levels, for decades. In addition to organizing, judging, and coaching, he's served on rules committees, steering committees, case writing committees. If half of us were a quarter as committed, Ethics Bowl would be ten times bigger already (forgive the hyperbolic math, but he deserves it!).

Why such extreme commitment? Because the transformative power and unique advantages of Ethics Bowl were obvious from the start, aligning perfectly with George's life purpose. Reflecting on the first Bowl he witnessed:

> I was amazed at the level of discussion and the depth of analysis… The ideas of thinking, rational analysis, and discussion seemed an unbeatable combination of skills valuable to citizenship. Most of my adult life has been focused on creating decent, responsible citizens, and the Ethics Bowl seemed to be a powerful approach to meeting my goals.

Rather than admiring from a distance, George has volunteered his time and lent his talents like few others, growing Ethics Bowl across age groups, formats, and locations. And despite retiring from his official teaching duties, he shows no sign of slowing.

Like other true believers, St. George has been forced to battle the naysayers, as well as his own less diplomatic instincts. And he has a simple yet effective response to those who challenge an ethics education's practical benefits.

> It turns out that many people, even in the world of Ethics Bowls, find my idealism disturbing. When I told my committee that I think the Ethics Bowl helps to create ethical citizens, several objected, one even sending me journal references that simply learning to think ethically does not guarantee people will act ethically. I had to engage in St. George style combat with my Dragon of Sarcasm not to reply. If a person never learns to think ethically, they never will. If they never learn rational discussion, they will never engage in rational discussion. Just because we cannot hit 100% ethical behavior is not a reason not to promote ethical thinking. Sadly, this person teaches ethics! Must be fun to be in his class.

There's a moral principle in there somewhere. Perhaps, "When an action has a reasonable chance of producing a morally praiseworthy outcome, one should try, absent compelling reasons, even if success isn't guaranteed."

Another principle we might intuitively endorse: "Leaders should encourage morally valuable activities." I bring this up because George makes a strong case that Ethics Bowl is far better at cultivating the type of person school systems claim to aspire to produce than many activities they fund as a matter of course.

> Early on in my adoption of the high school Ethics Bowl, we found research that showed if a student just witnessed an ethical discussion, they thought more ethically about the issue. Putting on my best Don Quixote attitude, I tried to convince the high school principals that Ethics Bowl was a more transformative experience than their sports teams. No spectator becomes a better basketball player by watching their high school team play. But that same student will become a better ethical thinker by watching a high school Ethics Bowl.

## Now That's Value

With all the extended benefits per investment buck, I've often wondered why philanthropists, nonprofits, and governments aren't throwing money at Ethics Bowl. Maybe they just don't know. But Jeanine DeLay with A2Ethics and the Michigan HSEB knows, and does a great job touting Ethics Bowl's affordability, allowing budget-strapped schools to launch and maintain them in spite of cuts.

Over the past few decades, K-12 education has faced many challenges, premiere among them, revenue losses. This situation has adversely impacted extracurricular programs, which in many places, now have fee or "pay-to-play" requirements. The advantages of Ethics Bowl are clear: it is neither facility nor equipment intensive, nor is it dependent on specialized or even developmental programs. The Bowl is also directly relevant to one of the central missions of schools: to educate students *how, but not what,* to think.

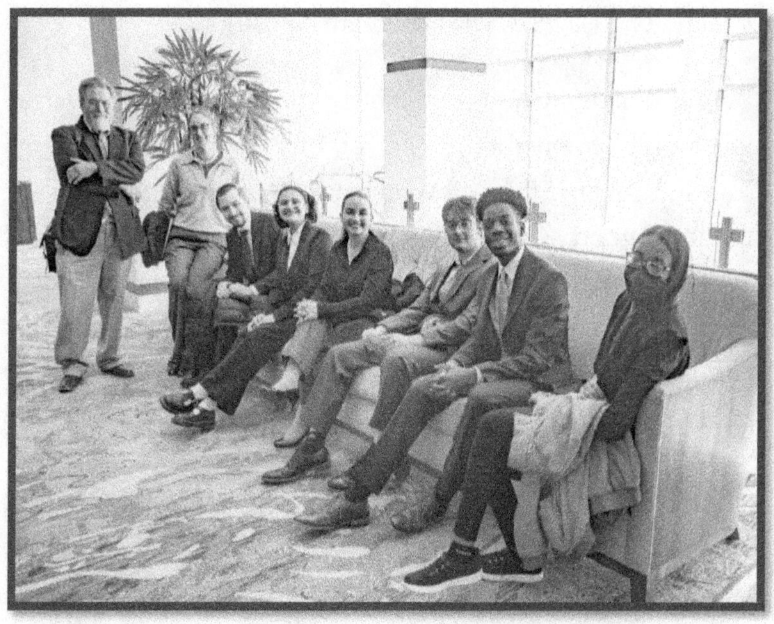

THE UNIVERSITY OF MARYLAND, BALTIMORE COUNTY IEB TEAM BETWEEN ROUNDS AT THE 2025 NATIONALS *COURTESY OF APPE IEB®*

Focusing on how to think rather than what to think allows Ethics Bowl to welcome participants, schools, volunteers, hosts, and sponsors of all stripes—no ideological litmus test required. For example, from PLATO's Middle School Ethics Bowl guidelines for judges:

> The main criterion for judging is to evaluate teams based on the quality of their thinking about a difficult ethical situation and their contribution to a reasoned and civil conversation… Judges should not engage a team in an argument based on a personal viewpoint nor score a team based on whether the judge agrees or disagrees with the team's position.

Directing judges to resist the temptation to score according to whether a team's views align with their own doesn't mean Ethics Bowl teaches that all arguments are equally good. Competition means standards, and Ethics Bowl affirms that moral arguments can be better or worse. But it does mean teams win rounds, events, and championships not by toeing a particular line, but by thoroughly and openly thinking through tough issues with sober humility.

In other words, there's no place for liberal, conservative, or any other sort of prejudice in Ethics Bowl. We're thoroughly independent. As I mentioned in chapters 4 and 5, and constantly remind myself in light of our sincere desire to invite anyone and everyone to join us, Ethics Bowl is ideologically neutral. However, this doesn't mean organizers lack settled views or that judges are indifferent pushovers. And while I am a fan of political philosopher John Rawls's Original Position thought experiment (look it up—maybe you'll become be a fan, too), this doesn't mean participants are expected to wipe their minds clean and reason from an unachievable, detached, omniscient perspective. It just means our allegiance as an institution is to clear moral reasoning, humility, collaboration, and not much else.

Besides, Ethics Bowlers quickly discover real issues are too complex to fit into neat left/right boxes. If you're skeptical, browse a case set. Any team that tried to force a single frame on topics that diverse and complicated would quickly discover how limited partisan thinking truly is.

## Thank You

If you're a current Ethics Bowl advocate, either by participating, coaching, organizing, moderating, judging, sponsoring or simply sharing it with friends, thank you. Future generations thank you. This generation thanks you. Lovers of justice, harmony, and mutual respect all over the world thank you.

If you're a debater, whether a participant, coach, organizer, host, judge, parent, or fan, thank you. We know your intentions are pure. We know debate helps young people overcome stage fright, build confidence, learn about important issues, and practice advocacy. But there's a superior alternative waiting, and the barriers to transition are virtually nonexistent.

In truth, you don't have to choose. Just as some kids play soccer in the fall then baseball in the spring, many teams alternate between debate and Ethics Bowl. I'd like to think most will come to prefer our model. But even if not, the experience will no doubt shape their attitudes, and in cases where we don't supplant debate, perhaps we can transform it from within. Infusing debate with Ethics Bowl's culture could produce similar benefits. And as a wise person once observed, it's amazing what you can achieve when you're unconcerned with who gets the credit.

THE 2024 IEB NATIONAL CHAMPS FROM THE UNIVERSITY OF NORTH CAROLINA AT CHAPEL HILL *COURTESY OF APPE IEB®*

Ethics Bowl currently doesn't offer as many opportunities to compete as debate, so that might be one reason why debate teams could be reluctant to fully commit to Ethics Bowl. It might also be reason for Ethics Bowl to expand offerings, reason for coaches to form standing ethics clubs and plan offseason scrimmages, reason for teams to look into Zoom-based events in other countries available year-round. (Hint: Ethics Olympiad.)

Ultimately, in a perfect world, Ethics Bowl would fully overtake debate. That's the goal. But one way for the debate community to save face, and for the Ethics Bowl community to more peacefully achieve its goals, could be a coexistence where debate becomes so much like Ethics Bowl, there's little reason to object to it.

## One Final Nudge

In the opening chapter, we considered Neil Howe's prediction that a galvanizing crisis will soon draw a bright line in history between everything that came before and everything that comes after. According to Howe, the bad news is that a terrible climax is inevitable. But the good news is that happy days are on the other side. He argues that if we agree that current conditions are unsustainable, we should anticipate the change with gladness, even if it will require a period of discomfort and pain.

> We are distressed because we have entered a season of history that we dread completing… a season of

> crisis likely to bring wrenching and unwanted changes to our lives. Yet on reflection we dread even more a future that is a linear extension of the past.

We dread a linear extension of the past because the division and rancor are only getting worse. But if Howe's cyclical theory of history is correct, and if change is inevitable, you might reason that rather than trying to save democracy or rescue the world, perhaps we should keep our heads down and mouths shut. Once the danger is over and sanity returns, then will be the time for the high-minded to ascend. Especially if it's going to take an event on the scale of the Great Depression or Civil War to break out of this funk, why expose ourselves? For now, just pretend to go along with the majority—whatever the majority happens to be where we live—and avoid the persecution we and our families might otherwise face.

I have to admit my risk averse instincts like this plan. And pretending to go along with the crowd is certainly doable. Pick any conflict in history. People found ways to side-step the craziness and enjoy quasi-normal, even thriving lives. Many regular Germans went about their business during the 1940s, reading books, learning to play instruments, shielding their families from the fervor and chaos around them. At least until it all came crashing down. Maybe that's exactly what you and I should do today—huddle around our loved ones, bury ourselves in hobbies, then push Ethics Bowl once things settle.

However, there is zero guarantee that things will turn out well. And given the stakes, passivity is not a defensible choice. We live under the specter of weapons of mass destruction, environmental degradation, AI misalignment and misuse. State and corporate surveillance are ever more invasive, media manipulation ever more sophisticated, and divisions sharper than in decades. To this already perilous mix, add a resurgence of nihilism and a creeping normalization of domestic military deployment. If ever there were a time for the ethically-minded to step up and take ownership of solutions, it's now.

We touched on Timothy Snyder's *On Tyranny* in chapter 9. He's the historian who studied democratic collapses into authoritarianism in Germany, Russia, Italy, and elsewhere, who urges us to demand that our leaders and media deal in facts. That way we're not snowed under by increasingly bolder and more dangerous lies. Snyder adds the importance of actively defending institutions like the courts and a free press, which "help us preserve decency." And he cautions us to suppress our inner pleaser—to never imagine what wannabe tyrants might want and preemptively accommodate their perceived wishes.

> In times like these, individuals think ahead about what a more repressive government will want and then offer themselves without being asked. A citizen who adapts in this way is teaching power what it can do.

Educators: we must keep this in mind as legislators and administrators hint that certain subjects should be avoided. If you're forced to choose between an environment of open inquiry or your livelihood, do what you must. We all have private responsibilities others are in no position to judge. But at least wait until you're forced. Do not proactively abdicate.

Channel the spirit of Socrates, who when facing execution essentially told those who attempted to suppress his philosophizing that they could piss right off.

> So long as I draw breath and have my faculties, I shall never stop practicing philosophy and exhorting you and elucidating the truth for everyone that I meet… Know that I am not going to alter my conduct, not even if I have to die a hundred deaths.[74]

For now, for most of us, our plight is far less dramatic. And if Socrates didn't back down when facing death, surely we can continue to fight the good fight when our pensions might eventually, one day, possibly be at slight risk (and at far less risk if we hold firm together). Case committees: keep those hot topics coming, thought police be damned. Let's enlighten as many as we can for as long as we can (in an age-appropriate way, of course). Because if not us, who?

74 From Plato's *Apology*, quoted in *The Consolations of Philosophy* by Alain De Botton, 2013.

Finally, Snyder reminds us of our power to inspire. For just as fear and conformity are contagious, so too are courage and principled defiance.

> Stand out. Someone has to. It is easy to follow along. It can feel strange to do or say something different. But without that unease, there is no freedom. Remember Rosa Parks. The moment you set an example, the spell of the status quo is broken, and others will follow.

It may be on the philosophers of the world—professional, part-time, and proudly amateur—to challenge emperors' nakedness for many years to come. But the good news is that while Ethics Bowl is immensely powerful, it's low-key. It's not like we're planning a coup and will be hanged if we fail. Just help expand and transition from traditional debate.

More Ethics Bowl means a citizenry less easily divided, less easily manipulated, and more inclined to seek objective justice with those they've been conditioned to hate. It means people more willing to rethink questionable commitments and to converge on policies that reflect our combined moral wisdom. Could there be a simpler way to make such a grand difference?

Buying in requires patience and justified hope. We can witness Ethics Bowl's impact immediately in our participants, yet it may take years to see a difference in our politics. When we do see it, it will be hard to prove Ethics Bowl was the cause. Yet most anything of value takes time, few things could be more valuable than such a fundamental transformation of hearts and minds, and so long as the improvements come, we should be unconcerned with whom or what gets the credit.

Remember, you have more power than you think. You can shape your community, your country, and your world one earnest, civil conversation at a time. And you can do it in a strategic, big picture, global movement fashion by playing whatever role you feel comfortable committing to. Remember Rutger Bregman's encouragement from *Moral Ambition* in chapter 1: we need all types. Every successful movement has. The only type we can't use is the Noble Loser who righteously complains without ever making a difference. Ethics Bowl empowers you to make a difference.

It's neither a magic bullet nor a sure thing. But with one solitary habitable planet, retreating to the shadows isn't a responsible option.

So join us, the thousands of organizers, coaches, judges, moderators, participants, sponsors, and fans who've decided this Ethics Bowl thing is worth a try. For the stakes are high and the hour is late. Yet it's Ethics Bowl to the rescue!

# ABOUT THE AUTHOR

Dr. Matt Deaton is the founder of EthicsBowl.org and author of six books including *Ethics in a Nutshell: The Philosopher's Approach to Morality in 100 Pages* available in PDF and audiobook at EthicsBowl.org/Resources. Thanks to the generous support of the Squire Family Foundation, he was the National High School Ethics Bowl's original Director of Outreach. He's the founder and original organizer of the Tennessee High School Ethics Bowl, co-founder and original co-organizer of the D.C. Area High School Ethics Bowl, and had a small hand in the creation of new Bowls all across the country, as well as the National High School Ethics Bowl itself. He's been a judge, a moderator, a case writer, a coach, and a trainer, and has worked with Ethics Bowlers and Ethics Olympiad *eth-letes* from elementary school through college.

He teaches philosophy and ethics at Pellissippi State Community College in Tennessee, where he took his very first philosophy and ethics classes, as well as remotely for the University of Texas at Tyler.

This fall he's coaching an Ethics Bowl team for the first time in a long time. Wish him luck!

SuperSocrates thanks you for reading. Now stop thinking about Ethics Bowl and go try it.

And if you enjoyed *Ethics Bowl to the Rescue!*, please tell a friend and write a brief review. Cheers!

www.ingramcontent.com/pod-product-compliance
Lightning Source LLC
Chambersburg PA
CBHW022045020426
42335CB00012B/550

* 9 7 8 1 9 5 1 6 7 7 1 6 9 *